Elections

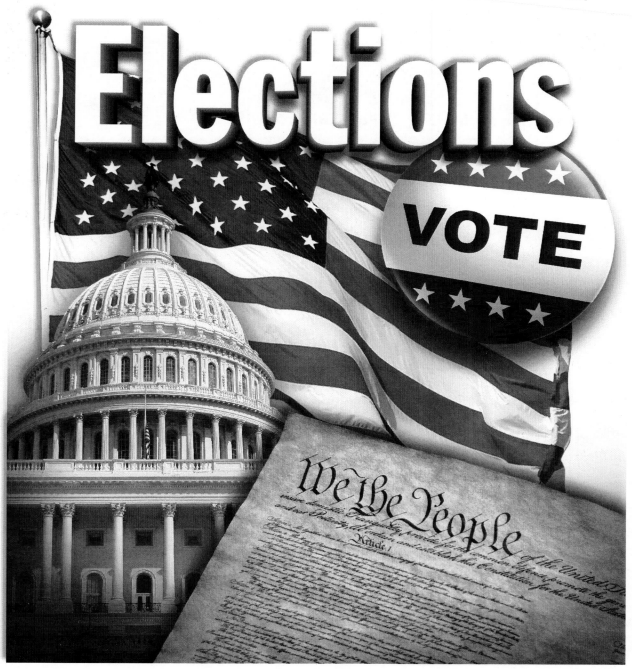

VOTE

Author

Kathy Kopp, M.S.Ed.

SHELL EDUCATION

Contributing Author

Christi Sorrell, M.A.Ed

Publishing Credits

Dona Herweck Rice, *Editor-in-Chief*; Robin Erickson, *Production Director*;
Lee Aucoin, *Creative Director*; Timothy J. Bradley, *Illustration Manager*;
Sara Johnson, M.S.Ed, *Senior Editor*; Evelyn Garcia, *Associate Education Editor*;
Stephanie Reid, *Cover Designer*; Corinne Burton, M.A.Ed., *Publisher*

Image Credits
P.23 Library of Congress [LC-DIG-ppmsca-25556];
p.45 Library of Congress [LC-D4-21198]; p.55 Library of Congress [LC-USZC2-2681];
p.67 Library of Congress LOC [LC-DIG-highsm-10103]; p.80 Library of Congress [LC-DIG-ds-00761]; p.91 Library
of Congress LOC [LC-USZ62-75334]; p.102 Library of Congress [LC-USZ62-761];
p.116 Library of Congress [LC-DIG-pga-01778]; p.129 The Granger Collection, New York/The Granger Collection;
all other images: Shutterstock.com

© 2004 Mid-continent Research for Education and Learning (McREL)
© 2007 Teachers of English to Speakers of Other Languages, Inc. (TESOL)

Shell Education
5301 Oceanus Drive
Huntington Beach, CA 92649-1030
http://www.shelleducation.com
ISBN 978-1-4258-0912-6
©2012 Shell Educational Publishing, Inc.

Table of Contents

The Importance of Civic Education

"Young people must learn how to participate in a democracy."
—*Constitutional Rights Foundation* 2000

It is the responsibility of those living in the United States to understand how civics relates to them. By being able to participate in a democracy, citizens can affect the nation and its well-being. Therefore, it is necessary for students to learn and understand civics. The National Council for the Social Studies (1994) states that "social studies programs should include experiences that provide for the study of the ideals, principles, and practices of citizenship in a democratic republic." By learning civics, students can be committed to addressing social and government issues in a constructive way. However, in order to do this, students must understand the country and communities in which they live.

According to the National Standards for Civics and Government (Center for Civic Education 1997, 141–145) the following are the organizing questions around which civic education should be based:

I. What are civic life, politics, and government?

II. What are the foundations of the American political system?

III. How does the government established by the constitution embody the purposes, values, and principles of American democracy?

IV. What is the relationship of the United States to other nations and to world affairs?

V. What are the roles of citizens in American democracy?

Teachers need to help students understand and respond to these civic questions so that students can apply their knowledge later in life when responding to daily events as adults in a democracy. Experiences during the K–12 school years lay the foundation for students to be able to evaluate situations and defend positions on public issues as well as influence civic life through working and managing conflict (Constitutional Rights Foundation 2000).

In 1998 and 2006, the National Assessment of Educational Progress assessed the civics achievement of students in fourth, eighth, and twelfth grades. "About two out of three American students at grades 4, 8, and 12 have at least a basic knowledge of civics," according to the 2006 test (Lutkus and Weiss 2007). The basic level on the test means students have a fundamental understanding of the civic education content for their grade levels. Further, the results from the 2006 test showed an increase in the fourth grade student scores since the test given in 1998. However, there was no significant change in the average scores at the eighth and twelfth grade levels (Lutkus and Weiss 2007).

The results of this assessment support the belief that civic education needs to be taught in different ways than it is currently being taught. Today's students no longer want to passively sit back and be told what to think. Instead, teachers should use simulations, creative thinking activities, primary sources, and other active learning strategies to help students better understand the country in which they live. This resource, *Elections*, uses all of these strategies to make learning more meaningful for students.

The Importance of Civic Education *(cont.)*

In 2000, the Center for Information and Research on Civic Learning and Engagement and the Carnegie Corporation of New York drew together a prestigious team of scholars and practitioners to create a report on civic education and young people. The report, titled *The Civic Mission of Schools*, was released in 2003 and advocates six approaches to increase the civic-mindedness of young people.

Elections utilizes four of these six approaches within the framework of the lesson plans available in this book. The approaches utilized in this resource include the following:

- providing classroom instruction in government, history, law, and democracy
- incorporating discussion of current, local, national, and international issues and events in the classroom
- encouraging student participation in school governance
- encouraging student participation in simulations of democratic process and procedures (Carnegie Corporation 2003)

The report states that by utilizing these approaches in the classroom, students gain more than simple enjoyment. Interesting lessons such as those in this book bring about the following benefits and skills:

- increased written and oral communication
- a working knowledge of government and democracy
- interest in current events
- a higher likelihood of consistent voting and voting on issues rather than personality when an adult

- increased ability to clearly articulate their opinions
- tolerance of differing opinions
- knowledge of how to make decisions even when others do not agree
- increased political and civic activeness as an adult
- appreciation of the importance and complexity of government
- increased civic attitude (Carnegie Corporation 2003)

All of these skills contribute to the goal of becoming a well-rounded, contributing, and responsible member of society outside of the classroom. However, these skills take time to develop and need to be integrated into the curriculum beginning in kindergarten and extending through twelfth grade to be ultimately effective (Quigley 2005). Therefore, teachers have a responsibility to students to provide them with the activities necessary to learn these skills. Utilizing the approaches advocated in *The Civic Mission of Schools* allows teachers the avenues through which to provide strong civic education.

The Importance of Civic Education *(cont.)*

In order for teachers to be effective, civic education needs to be recognized as a key aspect of today's curriculum.

Schools are the only institution with the capacity and mandate to reach virtually every young person in the country. Of all the institutions, schools are the most systematically and directly responsible for imparting citizen norms. Research suggests that children start to develop social responsibility and interest in politics before the age of nine. The way students are taught about social issues, ethics, and institutions in elementary school matters a great deal for their civic development (Kirlin 2005).

Civic education can be taught both formally and informally. Intentional formal lessons imbedded in the curriculum can give students a clear understanding of government and politics and the historical context for those ideas. This instruction should avoid teaching rote facts and give as much real-life context as possible. Informal curriculum refers to how teachers, staff, and the school climate can lead by example and illustrate to students how a working civic community operates (Quigley 2005). When adult role models portray and promote responsible civic engagement, students have a greater conceptual understanding of the formal, civic-based curriculum and how it relates to everyday life.

Using Current Events in Civic Education

Making curriculum relevant to the real world is a goal every teacher strives for, and civic education curriculum should be no different. Using current events in the classroom is one way to make real-world connections.

In a survey completed by the National Center for Education Statistics in 1997, students indicated that they were interested in news that pertained primarily to sports and entertainment. However, students who had taken courses in school that used current events outside of the sports and entertainment industries reported an increased interest in national issues.

Besides making curriculum relevant to students, using current events as part of civic education has other benefits as well. As this book illustrates, current events—such as elections—can be used as the basis for classroom discussions, debates, and cooperative learning activities, as well as magazine and newspaper articles about current events, which can serve as models for nonfiction writing. Students can also build vocabulary, language, reading comprehension, critical thinking and listening skills, and problem-solving strategies (Hopkins 1998). These higher-level thinking skills are important across all the content areas. Using current events in the classroom is an excellent curriculum model that allows teachers to successfully integrate the curriculum and make it meaningful to today's students.

Research-based Strategies for Teaching Civics

Using Simulations and Active Learning

When students experience an event, they are better able to remember that event. Simulations allow students to actively take part in concepts being taught. Simulations often reflect situations found in the real world. This book allows students to become part of the election process. By doing this, students will better understand and remember the concepts that are taught.

In an active learning classroom, teachers serve as facilitators of learning rather than the people who spoon-feed students the content. Andi Stix (2001) describes this change in the structure of the classroom in the following way:

Although the teacher maintains full control, the classroom becomes so highly structured that the teacher's position is elevated to the role of manager. Goals, objectives, and student outcomes continue to be firmly set by the teacher. However, the teacher now facilitates the class and helps students obtain those objectives through a process of discovery rather than through passive involvement.

Building Vocabulary

As Robert Marzano and his associates (2001b) note in the book *Classroom Instruction That Works*, students must encounter words multiple times before they can learn them. *Elections* repeats key vocabulary words throughout the lessons. Therefore, students encounter the same words even though new content is being taught. This helps students make multiple connections with the words and understand them through different contexts.

Marzano and his associates also note that seeing words before they appear in a reading passage can help students better learn the words. By completing the vocabulary activities prior to reading the background information, students are provided with the opportunity to learn and understand new words, thus helping with their comprehension of the background information when it is read. The vocabulary activities and the background information pieces give students a context for the words prior to the actual lesson.

Analyzing Primary Sources

Using primary sources gives a unique view of history that other ways of teaching history are unable to do. Primary sources include newspaper articles, diaries, letters, drawings, photographs, maps, government documents, and other items created by people who experienced events in the past firsthand. Primary sources show students the subjective side of history, as many authors that experienced the same event often retell it in completely different ways. These resources also show students how events affected the lives of those who lived them. Primary sources make history real to students. As students view these historical items, they are then able to analyze the events from various points of view and biases.

Research-based Strategies for Teaching Civics *(cont.)*

Analyzing Primary Sources *(cont.)*

This book allows students to evaluate a variety of primary sources. Each lesson contains a quotation, photograph, or document from election history. Students are asked questions and given activities to complete that will help them better understand the election process. Through these activities, students can place themselves in the past and analyze the historical process from various points of view.

Using Graphic Organizers

Graphic organizers are useful tools in helping students understand patterns, ideas, relationships, and connections. Nonlinguistic representation, such as graphic organizers, allows students to better recall the information they have learned (Marzano et al. 2001a).

The brain seeks patterns to make information meaningful (Olsen 1995). Graphic organizers assist students with these necessary connections. Graphic organizers also allow students to organize their thoughts as well as remember the information at a glance.

Research suggests that graphic organizers improve students' overall reading abilities. When graphic organizers are used, reading comprehension improves (Sinatra et al. 1984; Brookbank et al. 1999). In fact, the National Reading Panel (2000) included graphic organizers in its list of effective instructional tools to improve reading comprehension. Further, graphic organizers help students summarize information and create outlines for future writing assignments.

Graphic organizers are used throughout this book. Each lesson contains a graphic organizer that will allow students to summarize, judge, and analyze information given. The graphic organizers give the students the opportunity to think about and better understand the election process and how it relates to them.

Using Bloom's Taxonomy

In 1956, educator Benjamin Bloom worked with educational psychologists to classify levels of cognitive thinking. These six levels are *knowledge, comprehension, application, analysis, synthesis,* and *evaluation.* Bloom's Taxonomy has been used in classrooms for more than 50 years as a hierarchy that progresses from less to more complex. The progression allows teachers to identify the levels at which students are thinking. It also provides a framework for introducing a variety of questions and activities to all students.

The *knowledge* level asks students to recall information. The *comprehension* level asks students to understand and explain facts, often in their own words. The *application* level requires students to use prior knowledge to answer questions, transfer knowledge from one situation to another, and apply situations from the past to today or to themselves. The *analysis* level asks students to break down material and understand how parts relate to a whole. When students complete the *synthesis* level, they create new ideas based on the information they have learned or change ideas to make new ones. And, the *evaluation* level requires students to make judgments based on evidence or support ideas based on evidence given.

Research-based Strategies for Teaching Civics *(cont.)*

Using Bloom's Taxonomy *(cont.)*

Each lesson in this book includes a comprehension check in the form of an activity sheet that lists several activities for students to complete. The activities check for students' understanding in a way that will allow students to be challenged in their thinking. By assigning the various activities based on Bloom's Taxonomy, students can show their understanding of each concept in this book.

Extending Learning through Research

Allowing students to research information is an important skill at any level. And, with the Internet and other technology in classrooms today, it is a skill that students use often. This book allows students to research ideas and concepts based on each lesson. Students are asked to find facts about past elections and turn those facts into activities. The research extension ideas help students summarize information in fun and creative ways. These activities help students find main ideas, focus on key details, and break down ideas into their own thoughts, all of which are important reading comprehension skills. The research extension activities allow students to practice their reading and writing skills.

Making Connections

Students make meaning out of what is taught based on prior understanding, learning styles, and their own attitudes and beliefs. It is important when teaching any concept to help students make connections to themselves, to the past, or to the world in which they live. Many of the activities throughout this book provide students with opportunities to relate the ideas being taught to themselves. Students may be asked to become senators, presidents, or campaign managers. Then, as they research primary sources, they find the connections between past elections and elections today. Finally, as students learn about the election process in democracy, they understand the importance of participating in this process. By making connections, students can better understand and remember the concepts being taught.

Differentiating Activities

Classroom diversity exists throughout the country. Therefore, curriculum must also be diverse. This book provides opportunities for higher-level learners to be challenged, while also providing extra help for struggling students. Each lesson contains differentiation ideas. These ideas include activities for English language learners, below-grade-level learners, and above-grade-level learners, so that all students will be able to complete the simulation activities throughout the book.

Correlation to Standards

Shell Education is committed to producing educational materials that are research- and standards-based. In this effort, we have correlated all of our products to the academic standards of all 50 United States, the District of Columbia, the Department of Defense Dependent Schools, and all Canadian provinces. We have also correlated to the Common Core State Standards.

How to Find Standards Correlations

To print a customized correlation report of this product for your state, visit our website at **http://www.shelleducation.com** and follow the on-screen directions. If you require assistance in printing correlation reports, please contact Customer Service at 1-800-858-7339.

Purpose and Intent of Standards

Legislation mandates that all states adopt academic standards that identify the skills students will learn in kindergarten through grade twelve. Many states also have standards for Pre-K. This same legislation sets requirements to ensure the standards are detailed and comprehensive.

Standards are designed to focus instruction and guide adoption of curricula. Standards are statements that describe the criteria necessary for students to meet specific academic goals. They define the knowledge, skills, and content students should acquire at each level. Standards are also used to develop standardized tests to evaluate students' academic progress.

Teachers are required to demonstrate how their lessons meet state standards. State standards are used in development of all of our products, so educators can be assured they meet the academic requirements of each state.

McREL Compendium

We use the Mid-continent Research for Education and Learning (McREL) Compendium to create standards correlations. Each year, McREL analyzes state standards and revises the compendium. By following this procedure, McREL is able to produce a general compilation of national standards. Each lesson in this product is based on one or more McREL standards. The chart on the following page lists each standard taught in this product and the page number(s) for the corresponding lessons.

TESOL Standards

The lessons in this book promote English language development for English language learners. The standards listed on the following pages support the language objectives presented throughout the lessons.

Correlation to Standards (cont.)

McREL Correlation Chart

Page	Lesson Title	McREL Content Standard
16, 28, 39	Political Parties, The Presidential Election, State and Local Elections	Civics 25.2—Students know what constitutes political rights and why they are important
85	The History of Voting	Civics 24.1—Students know that a citizen is a legally recognized member of the United States who has certain rights and privileges and certain responsibilities
49, 60, 73	The Candidates, On the Campaign Trail, Making a Difference	Civics 28.2—Students know ways people can influence the decisions and actions of their government, such as voting; taking an active role in interest groups, political parties, and other organizations that attempt to influence public policy and elections; attending meetings of governing agencies; working on campaigns, circulating and signing petitions; taking part in peaceful demonstrations; and contributing money to political parties, candidates, or causes
109	Elected Leaders in Action	Civics 29.1—Students know what political leaders do and why leadership is necessary in a democracy
123	Doing My Part	Civics 29.2—Students know opportunities for leadership and public service in the student's own classroom, school, community, state, and the nation; and understand why leadership and public service are important to the continuance and improvement of American democracy
123	Doing My Part	Civics 29.3—Students understand the importance of individuals working cooperatively with their elected leaders
109	Elected Leaders in Action	Civics 29.4—Students know the major duties, powers, privileges, and limitations of a position of leadership, and knows how to evaluate the strengths and weaknesses of candidates in terms of the qualifications required for a particular leadership role
95	Going to the Polls	Civics 29.5—Students know qualities leaders should have, such as commitment to the values and principles of constitutional democracy, respect for the rights of others, ability to work with others, reliability or dependability, courage, honesty, ability to be fair, intelligence, willingness to work hard, and special knowledge or skills

TESOL Correlation Chart

Page	Lesson Title	TESOL Content Standard
60	On the Campaign Trail	2.1—Students will use English to interact in the classroom
16, 73	Political Parties, Making a Difference	2.2—Students will use English to obtain, process, construct, and provide subject matter information in spoken and written form
28, 39, 49, 85, 95, 109, 123	The Presidential Election, State and Local Elections, The Candidates, The History of Voting, Going to the Polls, Elected Leaders in Action, Doing My Part	2.3—Students will use appropriate learning strategies to construct and apply academic and knowledge

How to Use This Book

Lesson pacing in this book is very flexible. Each lesson is set up to be taught independent of the other lessons so that teachers can pick and choose just the topics they would like to cover. However, the lessons have been grouped into units, beginning with *What Is Politics?* and concluding with *After the Election*. Within each unit are two to three lessons connected to the unit title. If all lessons are completed in order, students will learn about the entire election process while participating in a mock election of their own.

The Lessons

Most lessons span two to three days. Each day's lesson is intended to take about 60 minutes of class time. The lessons involve the following main parts. Day One is an introduction to the content. This includes a short introductory activity, vocabulary, a reading selection with follow-up activity sheet, and primary source document with a follow-up activity sheet. Day Two begins the lesson's activity. Some activities may require more than one class session. If this is the case, the activity continues on Day Three. Additionally, students have an opportunity to demonstrate their understanding with a Comprehension Check at the end of each lesson. Each day's lesson plan includes step-by-step instructions to help you teach the lessons in a timely manner. The timeline on page 13 may help you plan each lesson.

- **Vocabulary activities** help students understand new words before delving into the background information.

- The **Background Information** page(s) include facts and information students need to fully understand each lesson's topic. Following each information sheet is a student activity sheet. This acts as a follow-up to the information presented in the text. It helps students understand the content within the text, and it holds them accountable for their reading.

- The **primary sources** introduce students to the past through pictures, quotes, documents, or maps. The student activity sheet that follows asks questions related to the primary source to check students' understanding of the document. It also establishes a connection to the lesson's topic.

- **Graphic organizers** are used on most of the activity sheets to help students better understand the topic at hand. The lessons include graphic organizers to check for understanding, help students organize their thoughts, or allow students to summarize information.

How to Use This Book (cont.)

The Lessons (cont.)

Timeline for Teaching the Lessons

Unit	Lessons	Timeline
Unit 1: What Is Politics?	Lesson 1: Political Parties	Day 1: Introduce the Content
		Day 2: Conduct and Assess
	Lesson 2: The Presidential Election	Day 1: Introduce the Content
		Day 2: Conduct and Assess
	Lesson 3: State and Local Elections	Day 1: Introduce the Content
		Day 2: Conduct and Assess
Unit 2: In the Running	Lesson 4: The Candidates	Day 1: Introduce the Content
		Day 2: Conduct and Assess
	Lesson 5: On the Campaign Trail	Day 1: Introduce the Content
		Day 2: Begin the Activity
		Day 3: Conclude and Assess
	Lesson 6: Making a Difference	Day 1: Introduce the Content
		Day 2: Begin the Activity
		Day 3: Conclude and Assess
Unit 3: Election Day	Lesson 7: The History of Voting	Day 1: Introduce the Content
		Day 2: Begin the Activity
		Day 3: Conclude and Assess
	Lesson 8: Going to the Polls	Day 1: Introduce the Content
		Day 2: Conduct and Assess
Unit 4: After the Election	Lesson 9: Elected Leaders in Action	Day 1: Introduce the Content
		Day 2: Conduct and Assess
	Lesson 10: Doing My Part	Day 1: Introduce the Content
		Day 2: Conduct and Assess

How to Use This Book *(cont.)*

Lesson Extensions

Differentiation Ideas

For each lesson, suggestions are given to help below-level students, above-level students, and English language learners. Extension ideas are also given to challenge more advanced students or those who finish early.

Research Extension Idea

A research extension idea is available in each lesson. These ideas allow students to further research some of the concepts or terms they have learned in the lesson. After researching, students are given activities to complete based on their research.

Connecting Elections

The lessons in this book mainly focus on the presidential elections. However, each lesson also contains a *Connecting Elections* section that will show students how all elections—from the local and state elections to the national elections—are connected in some way. It will also point out major differences among the various elections when applicable.

Student Activity Sheets

Every lesson contains reproducible student activity sheets that will aid in the teaching of the lesson. Some activity sheets involve maps, while others are lists or cards that students will use during the election simulation. Each lesson includes directions for the use of the activity sheets listed.

Comprehension Check

The Bloom's Taxonomy activities will check students' understanding of the lessons. The activities can be used in several different ways. The rubric on the following page can be used to help you grade this particular part of the lesson. Consider the following methods for assigning activities:

- Assign students activities according to their readiness levels.

- Assign a certain number of activities (such as three), but allow students to choose which activities they would like to do. You could leave this open to student choice, or you could require students to choose at least one activity from the higher-level group and leave the other two choices to them. Students may then choose two additional higher-level activities or they may choose to complete one lower-level and one additional higher-level activity or they may choose two lower-level activities.

- Write the activities on cubes and have the students roll them. The activities that the students roll are the ones they complete. Students may have two to three rolls, depending on how many activities you would like to have them complete.

How to Use This Book (cont.)

Comprehension Check (cont.)

Comprehension Check Evaluation Rubric			
Name _____			
	4 **Outstanding**	**3** **Good**	**2** **Fair**	**1** **Needs Work**
Completeness	All responses thoroughly complete the assignments.	Most responses complete the assignments, but they may not be thorough.	Some responses complete the assignments, but they may lack thoroughness.	Few or no responses complete the assignments, and they are not thorough.
Accuracy	All responses accurately and correctly provide the requested information.	Responses include mostly accurate and correct information.	Responses include somewhat accurate and correct information.	Responses include mostly inaccurate or incorrect information.
Organization	All responses are well organized, neat, and easily readable.	Responses are mostly organized and legible.	Responses are somewhat organized but may be somewhat illegible.	Responses are poorly organized and may be illegible.
Creativity	All responses are creative, interesting, and have a clear voice.	Responses are mostly creative and interesting but may lack a clear voice.	Responses may lack creativity, interest, and clear voice.	Responses lack creativity, interest and voice.
Vocabulary	All responses include adequate, specific vocabulary.	Most responses use adequate, specific vocabulary.	Some responses use specific vocabulary.	Responses use little to no specific vocabulary.
Appropriateness	All responses are appropriate to format.	Most responses are appropriate to format.	Some responses are appropriate to format.	Few or no responses are appropriate to format.
Conventions	Responses include few, if any, errors in grammar, punctuation, and spelling.	Responses include mostly correct grammar, punctuation, and spelling.	Responses include some incorrect grammar, punctuation, and spelling.	Responses include mostly incorrect grammar, punctuation, and spelling.

TOTAL: _____ / 28

Lesson 1: Political Parties

Standard

- Students know what constitutes political rights and why they are important (McREL Civics 25.2)

Vocabulary

- conservative
- Democratic Party
- government
- liberal
- political party
- Republican Party

Materials

- Half-sheet of 8.5" x 11" paper with the word *Democrat* written on it
- Half-sheet of 8.5" x 11" paper with the word *Republican* written on it
- *Political Parties Content-Area Vocabulary* (page 20)
- *Political Parties Background Information* (pages 21)
- *Political Parties Graphic Organizer* (page 22)
- *Political Parties Primary Source Connection* (pages 23–24)
- *My Party Candidate* (page 25–26)
- *Political Parties Comprehension Check* (page 27)
- Art supplies (e.g., poster boards, markers, rulers, glue)

 **Introduce the Content**

1. Divide the class into two groups. Give one group the half-sheet of paper with the word *Democrat* on it. Give the second group the half-sheet of paper with the word *Republican* on it. Assign one person in each group to be the recorder. This person should write down everyone's ideas related to each term. After a few minutes, have the groups trade papers. One person reads the other group's ideas related to the new term, and then the recorder adds any information the group believes was omitted. Share the two groups' ideas about both these political parties as a class.

2. Explain to students that they will learn about these two parties during their reading. Distribute copies of the *Political Parties Content-Area Vocabulary* activity sheet (page 20) to students. Discuss the definition of each term. Then, allow students to work with a partner to complete the activity sheet. You may also ask students to complete one of the following Vocabulary Extension Activities.

 # Lesson 1: Political Parties *(cont.)*

✔ Vocabulary Extension Ideas

- Divide the class into groups of three or four students. Have the groups discuss why they think there are just two main political parties in the United States. Have them postulate what a citizen does if he or she does not agree with either party on an issue.

- Ask students to create political picture dictionaries. Their dictionaries should include the vocabulary words, the definitions, and colorful pictures.

3. Distribute copies of the *Political Parties Background Information* activity sheet (page 21) to students. Have students read and discuss the information with a partner or in small groups. Distribute copies of the *Political Parties Graphic Organizer* activity sheet (page 22) to students and allow them to complete the activity sheet with their reading partner(s) based on the information they just read.

Differentiation Idea

English language learners may need additional help reading the background information. While other students are reading, work with these students in a small group. Help them understand and visualize the vocabulary terms.

4. Distribute copies of the *Political Parties Primary Source Connection* activity sheet (pages 23–24) to students. Discuss the picture and information as a class. Allow students to answer the questions in small groups. As an extension, ask them to do the primary source activity.

Differentiation Idea

English language learners may benefit from having specially chosen partners. Place them with students who are strong in English skills as well as those who have good historical understanding. English language learners can benefit from the other students' knowledge as they complete their primary source sheets and the other activities throughout the lesson.

 ## 2 Day Conduct and Assess

1. Begin with a review of political parties. Discuss the differences between the Republican and the Democratic parties. Have students use their *Political Parties Primary Source Connection* activity sheets to guide them.

2. Tell students that you are going to divide the class into two political parties. Divide one group into the Triangle Party and the other group into the Square Party.

3. Explain to students that each party will nominate a candidate for president, and that they will meet their candidate later. Today, they will learn how their candidate sides on the issues and will create a symbol to represent their party.

 # Lesson 1: Political Parties *(cont.)*

4. Distribute copies of the *My Party Candidate* activity sheet (pages 25–26) according to the two class party groups. Secretly, each group should review its candidate's beliefs regarding the issues and then think of a symbol to represent themselves based on this information.

5. Instruct students to work together to design and create a poster for their party. It should name their party and include a symbol. It can include information from the activity sheet. Explain that each student in the group should have a task to help create the poster.

Teacher Note: If students are really excited about this activity, allow them to take more than one day and have each group create a multimedia presentation. Allow the groups to then share their issues with the class.

6. Have each group present its finished poster to the other group.

7. Distribute copies of the *Political Parties Comprehension Check* activity sheet (page 27) to assess students' understanding of political parties. Use the Comprehension Check Evaluation Rubric (page 15) to evaluate students' work.

Extension Ideas

Find Out More

Post these questions and tasks at a literacy center for students to respond to. Provide the necessary resources for students to find out more about political parties.

- Who were the Democratic presidential candidates at the very start of the last presidential election?

- Who were the Republican presidential candidates at the very start of the last presidential election?

- Besides Democratic and Republican candidates, who else was on the ballot of the last presidential election, and what parties were they from?

- Has there ever been a president who was not from the Democratic or Republican party? If so, who?

- Who were some women who have run for president or vice president, and what parties were they from?

- Who has been a minority and has run for president or vice president, and what parties were they from?

 # Lesson 1: Political Parties *(cont.)*

☑ Research Extension

Have students choose one political party from American history other than the Democratic and Republican parties. Have them assemble a poster to tell about this party. Their posters should include: the party's slogan, the party's point of view on one or two issues of the time, the party's mascot or symbol, and pictures or illustrations of one or two candidates from this party, along with their names. Also, have students explain how this party influenced an election.

☑ Connecting Elections

Strict adherence to the beliefs of one political party can often be a problem. When one political party dominates Congress or the state legislatures, but the president or governors are from another party, these two branches often disagree. Have students reflect on and describe a personal experience when they were at odds with another person regarding a particular issue and they needed to compromise with that person or go along with his or her thinking.

Name: _____ Date: _____

Political Parties Content-Area Vocabulary

Directions: Read the definitions for each term. Use the definitions to help you complete each sentence using the terms.

> **conservative**—to be careful and avoid giving freely
>
> **Democratic Party**—the oldest political party in the United States, formed in 1792; one of the two main political parties today
>
> **government**—a system to rule a nation, state, town, or other group of people
>
> **liberal**—to be open-minded and to give away freely
>
> **political party**—a group whose members share the same ideas about government
>
> **Republican Party**—one of the two main political parties today; formed in 1854

1. Today, the United States has a two-party political system. The two parties are the _____ and the _____.

2. My mom works for the _____. She helps the mayor's office run the town.

3. When I go to vote, I will have to decide which _____ I want to belong to.

4. Mario has a much more _____ view of school rules. He would like to see them changed. He believes students should have more choices.

5. Anisha is much more _____ than Mario. She likes the school rules the way they are. She thinks each person should be responsible to follow the rules.

Name: _____ Date: _____

Political Parties Background Information

Directions: Read the information below.

Political parties first began in 1796. Our country was new. The **government** had just started. People joined political parties. They had ideas about how the government should work. They joined other people who had the same ideas. Most of the ideas were about how the government should work.

The first two parties were the Federalists and the Anti-Federalists. The Federalists believed in a strong national government. They wanted it to be powerful. They wanted it to be in control.

The Anti-Federalists were another party. They did not want a strong national government. They wanted each state to run itself. They thought citizens should watch over the people who ran the government. They did not want leaders to have too much power. They thought all people should help run the government.

Party names and ideas have changed over the years. Today, we have two major parties. They are the Democratic and Republican parties.

The **Democratic Party** is said to be **liberal**. This means that they like to give freely. They also believe in a strong government. Their website says that the party wants to keep our nation safe. They want to grow opportunities for every person. They support strong economic growth. They work toward affordable health care for all citizens. Democrats support social groups. This means that the government gives to people in need. Their symbol is the donkey.

The **Republican Party** started in 1854. This party started over slavery. They did not want it to spread into new states. Abraham Lincoln was the first Republican to be elected president. Republicans are said to be **conservative**. This means that they are careful about giving things away freely. Their website tells what they believe. They believe that the strength of our country lies with the people. They believe that each person should be responsible for himself. They also believe that the government should be careful with money. And, people should be able to keep more of the money they earn. Government should only give services that cannot be done by the people. They say that we should value and preserve our national strength and pride. They also say that we should share peace, freedom, and human rights all around the world. Their symbol is the elephant.

There are a lot of smaller parties, too. Sometimes, a third person will run in an election. This person is not a Republican. This person is not a Democrat. He or she belongs to a third party. These parties have ideas that are important to a lot of people. Third parties give citizens more choices. This is helpful when they do not agree with the two main political parties. These third-party candidates often do not win enough votes to win elections. Ross Perot ran for president as an independent in 1992. He gained many votes but did not win.

Name: _____ Date: _____

Political Parties Graphic Organizer

Directions: Use the information from the *Political Parties Background Information* activity sheet to compare Democrats to Republicans.

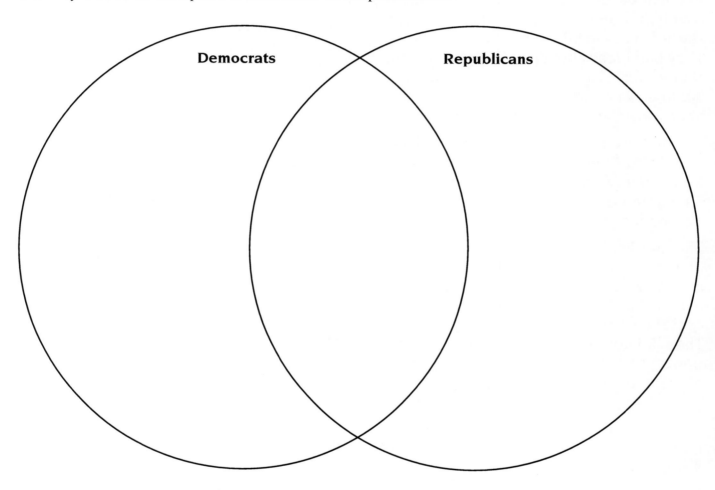

Democrats   Republicans

1. Would you say today's Democratic Party is more like the Federalists or Anti-Federalists? Explain your answer.

_____

_____

_____

Name: _____ Date: _____

Political Parties Primary Source Connection

Directions: Read the information below.

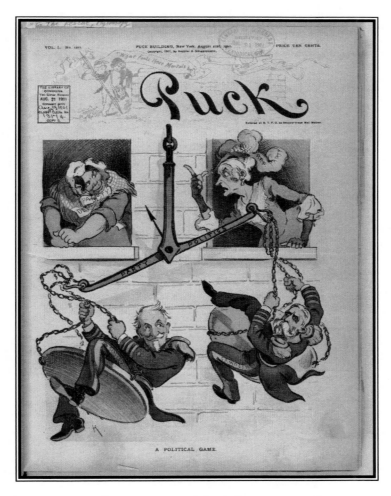

Primary Source Background Information

This is a political cartoon from 1901. It is titled "A Political Game." It shows two women leaning out windows. The woman on the left is Irish and looks poor (or does not look wealthy). She represents the Democratic Party. The older woman on the right is well-dressed. She represents the Republican Party. The balance scale between them represents party politics. Rear Admiral Winfield S. Schley is on the left. He is trying to upset the balance by pulling on the chains. This causes the scale to swing wildly. Admiral William T. Sampson is on the right. He is trying to hang on.

Political Parties Primary Source Connection *(cont.)*

Primary Source Questions

Directions: Use the information from the *Political Parties Primary Source Connection* activity sheet. Think about the political cartoon. Answer the questions below.

1. Describe what each woman might be thinking.

The Irish woman on the left might be thinking…

_____

_____

The older woman on the right might be thinking…

_____

_____

2. Who looks to be "tipping the scale" in his favor? What do you think this means?

_____

_____

3. Do you think the political scale will ever be balanced? Explain your answer.

_____

_____

Primary Source Extension

How do you think this cartoon applies to today's political parties? Find out about one issue the two parties disagree over. Show each party's ideas about this issue on a separate sheet of paper folded in half. Write and draw what a Democrat might believe about this issue on the left side. Write and draw what a Republican might believe about this issue on the right side.

Name: _____ Date: _____

My Party Candidate

Directions: Use this information to create a symbol for your political party. You can use what you learn about your candidate here to create a poster to advertise your party. Include your party name, symbol, and information about these issues.

Square Party

This candidate believes that in the lunchroom:

1. Students should have assigned seats. This way, the lunchroom monitor can keep careful track of everyone.

2. Food prices should be different for different students. Some students should pay more and some students should pay less. The price should depend on whether they can pay or not.

3. Students should not have access to vending machines. This way, the principal can be sure no junk food is available to students.

This candidate believes that on the soccer field:

1. All children should be able to play, no matter how good or how bad they are.

2. Each team should have many coaches. The league should pick all the coaches.

3. Anyone who wants to come watch a game should be able to do so, free of charge.

4. The league should rely on local tax dollars to pay for uniforms, grounds keeping, and so on.

My Party Candidate *(cont.)*

Directions: Use this information to create a symbol for your political party. You can use what you learn about your candidate here to create a poster to advertise your party. Include your party name, symbol, and information about these issues.

Triangle Party

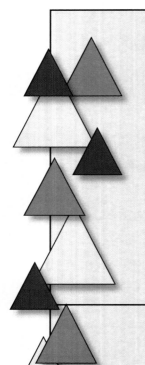

This candidate believes that in the lunchroom:

1. Students should be able to roam the cafeteria freely. This way, they can visit with many friends instead of just one or two.

2. Food prices should change based on how much food costs that week, and how many students buy lunch each week. The lunchroom should charge everyone the lowest price possible. Everyone should pay the same price for lunch.

3. Students should have access to vending machines. They give students more choices.

This candidate believes that on the soccer field:

1. Each team should have try-outs. Only the best players should be chosen to play on the team.

2. Each team should have one or two coaches. The teams should pick the coaches.

3. For people who want to watch the games, the league should charge a fair price for admission. This will raise money for the league. They will not have to rely on tax dollars to fund this fun sport.

Name: _____ Date: _____

Political Parties Comprehension Check

Directions: On a separate sheet of paper, answer the questions below according to the directions from your teacher.

★ Remember

List the two main political parties today.

★ Understand

Compare the Republican Party to the Democratic Party. Include at least two details about each party.

★ Apply

Political parties began because many people had different ideas about how the government should be formed. Write about a time when you disagreed with someone over how something should go. Perhaps it was a game. Perhaps it was a restaurant choice. Include dialogue between you and the person you disagreed with.

★ Analyze

Why is it important for parties to tell about their beliefs? Explain what might happen if parties did not share their beliefs.

★ Evaluate

List five important issues in the news today. Then, rate each one on a scale of 1–5, with one being the most important issue to today's political parties. Next to each rating, explain why you rated it the way you did.

★ Create

The symbol for the Democratic Party is the donkey. The symbol for the Republican Party is the elephant. Choose one party. Create a new symbol for this party. Explain why you chose this symbol.

 # Lesson 2: The Presidential Election

Standard

- Students know what constitutes political rights and why they are important (McREL Civics 25.2)

Vocabulary

- Constitution
- eligible
- qualify
- term

Materials

- The Presidential Election Content-Area Vocabulary (page 32)
- The Presidential Election Background Information (page 33)
- The Presidential Election Graphic Organizer (page 34)
- The Constitution Rules Primary Source Connection (pages 35–36)
- Who Is Eligible? (page 37)
- The Presidential Election Comprehension Check (page 38)
- Three note cards per pair of students

 ## Introduce the Content

Day 1

1. If students did not participate in the previous lesson, discuss political parties with them. Ask students to think about the current president and vice president. List their names on the board. Have students discuss with a partner the steps they think these people took to become elected as our national leaders. Ask volunteers to share their ideas with the class.

2. Tell students that not just anyone can run for the office of president and vice president. Each person must *qualify* to be *eligible* to run. Discuss as a class the meanings of these two words. Also ask students to predict what the qualifications might be.

3. Distribute copies of *The Presidential Election Content-Area Vocabulary* activity sheet (page 32). Have students discuss the terms with a partner and reflect on the class discussion to complete the page collaboratively. You may also ask that they complete a Vocabulary Extension Activity with their partners.

Differentiation Idea

Work with **English language learners** to ensure that the vocabulary is clear to them. If necessary, look up the vocabulary words with them and discuss the words in context.

Lesson 2: The Presidential Election *(cont.)*

☑ Vocabulary Extension Activities

- Ask students to look at the vocabulary words. Then, have them explain ways that each word applies to a president and a vice president. They can show their explanations on note cards.

- Have each student pretend he or she wants to run for president. Then, ask students to create a short speech announcing their interest. Students should use all four vocabulary words in their speeches.

4. Distribute copies of *The Presidential Election Background Information* (page 33) and The Presidential Election Graphic Organizer (page 34) activity sheets. Have students read the information with their partners. Then, have the partners write three important facts from the information, each on its own note card. Collect the cards to use as a review at the beginning of Day 2.

Differentiation Idea

List the qualifications for president and vice president on sentence strips. Meet with **English language learners** in a small group. Have them read each qualification, and sort them into two categories: those for president and those for vice president.

5. Ask students to complete the graphic organizer with their reading partner. Once students have completed the work, conduct a class discussion to compare the information. Use the following discussion questions:

- What are the qualifications to run for president?

- What are the qualifications to run for vice president?

- Which position has stricter qualifications? Why do you think this is?

- What are the two term restrictions? Why are there two?

6. Distribute copies of *The Constitution Rules Primary Source Connection* activity sheet (pages 35–36) to students. As a class, read about the 22nd Amendment to the Constitution aloud. Then, ask students to answer the questions that follow.

7. Have students discuss their answers in small groups. For further comprehension, ask them to complete the Primary Source Extension activity.

Lesson 2: The Presidential Election *(cont.)*

 ## Conduct and Assess

1. Use students' fact cards to conduct a review of the information from Day 1. Divide students into pairs. Randomly distribute three fact cards to each pair of students. Have them read and discuss the information on the cards. Then, have them pass the cards to the partners on their right. Have the pairs read and discuss this second set of cards, then pass them one more time. As a class, ask for volunteers to summarize the information the students learned the previous day.

2. Divide students into five or six groups. Give each group a copy of the *Who Is Eligible?* activity sheet (page 37). Read the directions to the class. Explain that a potential candidate is one who may possibly run, but is not in the running yet. Read about the first candidate together, and decide whether he can run and why. Then, have the groups work collaboratively to finish the activity sheet. As a class, summarize whether each potential candidate is eligible to run for his or her respective office.

3. Distribute *The Presidential Election Comprehension Check* activity sheet (page 38) to assess students' understanding of national elections. Use the Comprehension Check Evaluation Rubric (page 15) to evaluate students' work.

Extension Ideas

 ### Find Out More

Post this question at a literacy center for students to respond to. Provide the necessary resources for them to find out the answer to this situation.

- What might happen if the vice president has to take over as president, but he or she is not old enough, according to the Constitution. For example, say a vice president is 32 years old. Then, he must take over as president. The president is supposed to be at least 35! Write what you think would happen. Then, find out if you are right. Explain why you were right or wrong.

Research Extension

The president and vice president make up the executive branch of our government. But, citizens also elect senators and representatives from each state. They make up the legislative branch of government. Have students conduct research to find out if the Constitution lays out qualifications for them, too. Students can find out how long each term is, how many terms they can serve, or if there are limits. Have students summarize this information in a T-chart.

Lesson 2: The Presidential Election *(cont.)*

Differentiation Idea

As an extension, ask **above-grade-level** students to research specific senators or representatives from history. In their research, ask them to find out how these people qualified for their office, and how long they served in this office.

✔ Connecting Elections

Some rights and privileges of citizens have rules, too. For example, people must be at least 16 years old to drive in most states. People must be at least 18 years old to vote. Children must be five years old to go to school. Have students think of a time when they or someone they know qualified or did not qualify to participate in a special event. They should explain what the event was, and why the person did or did not qualify to participate.

Name: _____ Date: _____

The Presidential Election Content-Area Vocabulary

Directions: Write the vocabulary term next to its definition. Choose terms from the box below.

| Constitution | eligible | qualify | term |

Vocabulary Term	Definition
1.	to be able to run for political office
2.	the laws written to show how the government will run
3.	the length of time of a political office
4.	to meet the rules to run for political office

Directions: Illustrate each term in the spaces below.

Constitution	eligible
qualify	**term**

Name: _____ Date: _____

The Presidential Election Background Information

People in the United States have political rights. This means that they can take part in politics. Voting is one way to participate. Seeking and holding public office is another way. One public office is president. Every four years, voters go to the polls. They cast their vote for their next president. But, not everyone can run for president. There are rules to follow. These rules come from our Constitution. All presidential candidates must follow these rules. They must **qualify** to run for president.

How to Qualify

People first decide to run for president. Most belong to a political party. They must have the support of their party. Getting elected takes a lot of teamwork! They check to be sure they are **eligible** to run. They look to the Constitution. This tells how our government works. One part tells what must be true for a person to be a presidential candidate. The person must be a natural-born citizen of the United States. This means that this person was born here. The person must be at least 35 years old. And, this person must have been a resident of the United States for the past 14 years. For example, a person could not have lived in another country five years ago, or even ten years ago.

The person must have called the United States home for the past 14 years or more.

The presidential candidate picks a vice-presidential candidate. This is his or her running mate. This person must qualify, too. This person does not have to be a natural-born citizen. But, he or she must have lived here for seven or more years. This person must also be 30 years old or more. And, the presidential candidate and his or her running mate may not live in the same state.

The Term of Office

A president leads the United States for one **term**. This is four years. This is why we have elections every four years. The Constitution outlines the term of the office of president. A person can only serve two terms. This adds up to eight years. Or, a person can be president for up to ten years. How can that be? Some presidents take office in the middle of a term. This might happen if a president dies in office or leaves for some reason. This new president must add these years to an elected term. So, if a person takes over for three years, he or she can only run once. Another four-year term would be too many years as president.

Name: _____ Date: _____

The Presidential Election Graphic Organizer

Directions: Compare the qualifications for the office of president and vice president. Use information from *The Presidential Election Background Information* activity sheet to help you. Then answer the questions below.

President	Vice President

1. What are two political rights of American citizens?

_____

2. Why do you think the Constitution explains the qualifications for president and vice president?

_____

_____

3. Do you think the qualifications for the offices are fair? Explain why you think this.

_____

_____

Name: _____ Date: _____

The Constitution Rules Primary Source Connection

Directions: Read the information below.

Excerpt from The Constitution of the United States

U.S. Constitution—Amendment 22

Section 1.

No person shall be elected to the office of the President more than twice, and no person who has held the office of President, or acted as President, for more than two years of a term to which some other person was elected President shall be elected to the office of the President more than once. But this Article shall not apply to any person holding the office of President, when this Article was proposed by the Congress, and shall not prevent any person who may be holding the office of President, or acting as President, during the term within which this Article becomes operative from holding the office of President or acting as President during the remainder of such term.

Section 2.

This article shall be inoperative unless it shall have been ratified as an amendment to the Constitution by the legislatures of three-fourths of the several States within seven years from the date of its submission to the States by the Congress.

Primary Source Background Information

The United States Constitution has had many changes. These are called *amendments*. The 22nd Amendment limits the terms for the president. Congress passed this amendment on March 21, 1947. Then, a majority of states had to vote to accept it. It was ratified, or approved to be added, on February 27, 1951.

Name: _____ Date: _____

The Constitution Rules Primary Source Connection *(cont.)*

Primary Source Questions

Directions: Think about the 22nd amendment. Then answer the questions below.

1. Explain your thoughts about the 22nd Amendment as you read it.

_____

_____

2. Why do you think this amendment was important in 1947?

_____

_____

3. Do you think this is an important amendment today? Explain your answer.

_____

_____

_____

_____

Primary Source Extension

Find out about one constitutional amendment that came *before* the 22nd, and one that came *after* the 22nd Amendment. On a separate sheet of paper, prepare a summary of this information. Tell the number of the amendment, when it was ratified, and how it changed the Constitution.

Name: _____ Date: _____

Who Is Eligible?

Directions: These people all want to run for president or vice president. Read the information about each potential candidate. Then, decide whether he or she is eligible to run for that office.

James West

James wants to run for president of the United States. He is 45 years old. He was born in Canada. He lived in Michigan for most of his life. He has lived in Illinois for the past 15 years.

Can James run for president of the United States? (circle one)   yes   no

Why or why not? _____

_____

Cindy East

Cindy wants to run for vice president of the United States. She is 30 years old. She was born in England. She grew up in France. Then she moved to Virginia to go to college. She has lived there for the past 12 years.

Can Cindy run for vice president of the United States? (circle one)   yes   no

Why or why not? _____

_____

Gerald North

Gerald wants to run for vice president of the United States. He is 55 years old. He was born in California. He spent most of his life there. Then he took a job in China. He moved back to the States five years ago. Now he works in Texas.

Can Gerald run for vice president of the United States? (circle one)   yes   no

Why or why not? _____

_____

Vera South

Vera wants to run for president of the United States. She is 70 years old. She was born in New York. She grew up in Australia. Her family moved to New Jersey when she was five years old. She has lived there ever since.

Can Vera run for president of the United States? (circle one)   yes   no

Why or why not? _____

_____

Name: _____ Date: _____

The Presidential Election Comprehension Check

Directions: On a separate sheet of paper, answer the questions below according to the directions from your teacher.

★ Remember

List the qualifications for president and vice president.

★ Understand

Draw a picture of a possible presidential or vice presidential candidate. Use your vocabulary terms. Label your picture to show how the terms are related to the possible candidate.

★ Apply

If you could interview the president or vice president, what questions would you ask about his or her qualifications? Write a list of three interview questions. Then, write how the president or vice president might respond. Be sure he or she meets each quality!

★ Analyze

If you had written the Constitution, what qualifications would you have included for president and vice president? Write a list of new or different qualifications.

★ Evaluate

Do you think the terms and qualifications for each office are fair? Why or why not? Explain your answer in a letter to Congress, stating whether or not they should change or keep the current qualifications. Justify your position.

★ Create

Suppose you would like to run for president, but you are an immigrant who has just become a citizen. Therefore, you realize you will never be able to do this. Write a letter to Congress stating why this qualification is unfair. Then, respond as a congressman/woman stating why that qualification is necessary and fair.

Lesson 3: State and Local Elections

Standard

- Students know what constitutes political rights and why they are important (McREL Civics 25.2)

Vocabulary

- citizen
- governor
- mayor
- office
- representative
- senator

Materials

- *State and Local Elections Content-Area Vocabulary* (page 42)
- *State and Local Leaders Background Information* (page 43)
- *State and Local Leaders Graphic Organizer* (page 44)
- *Mayor's Parade Primary Source Connection* (pages 45–46)
- *My State and Local Leaders* (page 47)
- *State and Local Elections Comprehension Check* (page 48) (*optional*)
- Internet access for students to research state and local officials

 ## Introduce the Content

1. If you have not completed the previous lessons, discuss the two main political parties in the United States, and how the president gets elected.

2. Begin the day by writing the words *state leaders* and *local leaders* on the board. Have students turn to a partner to discuss who these people might be, and to list any examples they can think of.

3. As a class, explain that state leaders work in the state capital. They are governors, state senators, and state representatives. Explain that local leaders work in a city or district. They are mayors, city councilmen, the superintendent of schools, the sheriff, and so on. Explain that most state leaders are elected, but some local leaders are appointed.

Differentiation Idea

Before the brainstorming activity, explain to **English language learners** the difference between a state and a local government. Give them examples. This will help them to understand the vocabulary, and allow them to participate in the brainstorming activity.

 # Lesson 3: State and Local Elections *(cont.)*

4. Distribute copies of the *State and Local Elections Content-Area Vocabulary* (page 42) activity sheet. Have students discuss the terms with a partner and reflect on the class discussion to complete the page collaboratively. You may also ask that they complete a Vocabulary Extension Activity with their partners as well.

✔ Vocabulary Extension Activities

- Ask each student to find a news article about a state or local politician. Have the students review their articles, creating summaries that explain what the politician did. In their summaries, ask students to use at least three vocabulary words.

- Have students find pictures of their mayors and governors. Ask them to write captions below the pictures. Each caption should contain one vocabulary word.

5. Distribute copies of the *State and Local Leaders Background Information* (page 43) and *State and Local Leaders Graphic Organizer* (page 44) activity sheets to students. Read and discuss the information as a class. Have students complete this activity sheet independently.

Differentiation Idea

Meet with **below-level** students and **English language learners** as a group to review the information on the activity sheet. Encourage them to highlight any information they feel should be included in the graphic organizer.

6. Distribute the *Mayor's Parade Primary Source Connection* activity sheet (pages 45–46) to students. Discuss the photograph and information with the class. As a class, discuss what other duties and responsibilities a mayor might have. Share a local newspaper article summary that involves the mayor. Finally, discuss and complete the questions as a class.

 # Conduct and Assess
Day 2

1. Begin the day by reviewing the graphic organizer students completed the previous day. Discuss some similarities and differences between state and local leaders.

2. Distribute the *My State and Local Leaders* activity sheet (page 47) to students. Ask if students know the names of the present governor and lieutenant governor. Then, use the Internet to display this information for students to write on their page. Repeat this step for other local elected positions. Allow students to write questions they would ask the governor and mayor, and encourage them to share their answers with the class.

Lesson 3: State and Local Elections *(cont.)*

Differentiation Idea

Have **above-level** students find out who other elected officials are. Have them research who they are and what position they serve. They can also find out how long each term lasts, and if there are term limits. Have students organize this information on a poster to share with the class.

3. Distribute copies of the *State and Local Elections Comprehension Check* activity sheet (page 48) to assess students' understanding of national elections. Use the Comprehension Check Evaluation Rubric (page 15) to evaluate students' work.

Extension Ideas

✔ Find Out More

Explain that each person who runs for office belongs to a political party. Have students find out whether their governor, lieutenant governor, and mayor are Democrats, Republicans, or if they belong to another party.

✔ Research Extension

As an extension idea, allow students to research governors, mayors, or other local and state officials who went on to run for a national office. Have them create lists of these politicians. They should include where these politicians' political careers began and where their political careers ended.

✔ Connecting Elections

Have students think about their school principal. Have them compare the office of mayor and the role of school principal in a Venn diagram. Then, have students decide whether a mayor and principal are more alike or more different and explain their reasoning.

Name: _____ Date: _____

State and Local Elections Content-Area Vocabulary

Directions: Write the vocabulary term next to its definition. Use all the terms from the box below and then answer the questions.

citizen	governor	mayor
office	representative	senator

	Vocabulary Word	Definition
1.		a member of state and national government; part of the Senate
2.		a member of a state or national government; part of the House of Representatives
3.		the leader of a city or town
4.		the leader of a state
5.		a position of authority, as in government
6.		a person who lives in a city, state, or nation

Directions: Finish the sentences. Use one term from the word box in each blank.

7. The _____ of the state of Ohio had just been elected to this _____.

8. The town had to have a special election. The _____ elected a new _____.

9. The _____ and _____ work very hard with the president and vice president to help run the country.

Name: _____ Date: _____

State and Local Leaders Background Information

You know that the president leads the United States. He or she works with the vice president. They also work with people who work for each state. These people are called **senators** and **representatives**. They work for their state. But they do their work in Washington, DC. They work in a building called the Capitol.

State Leaders

Each state has its own government. It is a lot like our national government. But, there is no president for your state. The leader of your state is called the **governor**. This person works with the lieutenant governor. This person is kind of like the vice president. They work together to run the state.

The governor must be eligible to run for this office. But, the qualifications in each state are different. In some states, the governor serves a four-year term. In other states, he or she only serves a two-year term. In some states, the governor can serve as many terms as he or she wants. In other states, the number of terms for the governor is limited. To serve as governor, a candidate must be a certain age or older. Most governors must be **citizens** of the United States. And, they must be citizens of their state for so many years. But, every state is different.

Citizens of the United States elect the president. These same citizens elect the governor, too. They vote for the governor of their own state. A person from Texas cannot vote for the governor of Ohio.

The governor works with state senators and state representatives. These people are like the national leaders. But, they work in the state capital. They do not work in Washington, DC.

Local Leaders

Your city has many local leaders. They might be elected, too. The **mayor** is one local elected official. The mayor is the leader of a city. A person must qualify to run for mayor. Every state has different rules about this, just like the governor. Mayors are elected by the citizens of their towns. A person from one town cannot vote for the mayor in another town.

Other local **offices** might be your city council. They might be your school's parent-teacher association (PTA). They might be members of your district's school board. There are student elections in schools, too. Citizens can elect many people to office. Some are local. Some work for their state. And some work for the nation.

Name: _____ Date: _____

State and Local Leaders Graphic Organizer

Directions: Use the information from the *State and Local Leaders Background Information* activity sheet to write at least three details about state leaders and at least three details about local leaders.

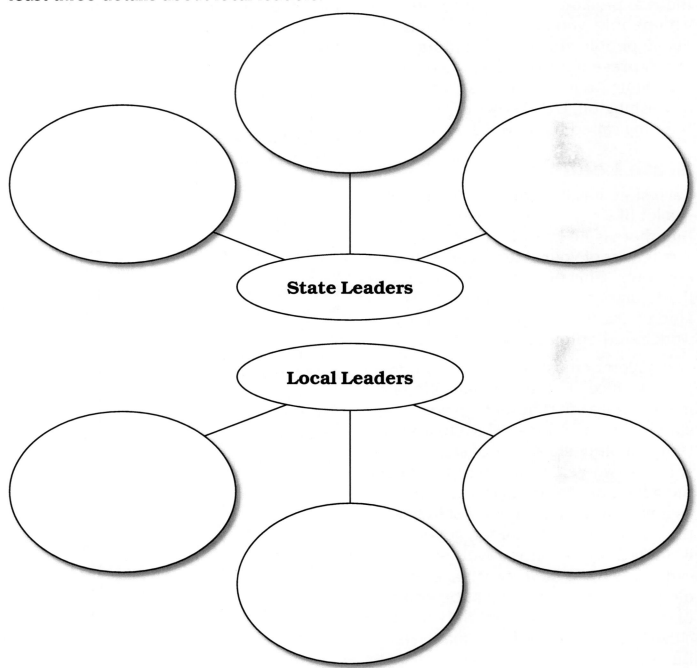

Name: _____ Date: _____

Mayor's Parade Primary Source Connection

Directions: Read the information below.

021198- ADMIRAL DEWEY AND MAYOR VAN WYCK, DEWEY LAND PARADE.

Primary Source Background Information

Mayors take part in ceremonies. They represent the city. This mayor was in New York City. His name is Mayor Van Wyck. He was leading the Dewey Land Parade on September 30, 1899. The other person in the carriage is Admiral Dewey. He was a naval officer. Admiral Dewey was a hero. He fought in the Spanish-American War. He won the Battle of Manila Bay without losing one single solider from his troop.

Name: _____ Date: _____

Mayor's Parade Primary Source Connection *(cont.)*

Primary Source Questions

Directions: Look at the picture. Answer the questions below.

1. Why was the mayor in the carriage leading the parade?

_____

_____

2. How can you tell that this parade was special?

_____

_____

3. Why is the office of mayor an important one?

_____

_____

Primary Source Extension

- On a separate sheet of paper, write a journal entry as if you were one of the parade watchers. Describe the scene, how everyone felt, and why this was a memorable event.

- Leading parades is just one duty of a mayor. Find out what else a mayor does. What are his duties and responsibilities in your city? Who is your mayor? Find out the answers to these questions. Make a picture book illustrating and explaining the duties and responsibilities of your town mayor.

Name: _____ Date: _____

My State and Local Leaders

Directions: Find out who your state and local leaders are. Use the Internet or information from your elections office or local library.

1. I live in the state of _____ .

2. The governor of my state is _____ .

3. The lieutenant governor of my state is _____ .

4. I live in the town of _____ .

5. The name of my town's mayor is _____ .

6. This is one other locally elected office. _____

7. This person holds this office right now. _____

8. If I could ask my governor one thing, I would ask _____

_____

_____

_____

9. If I could ask my mayor one thing, I would ask _____

_____

_____

_____

Name: _____ Date: _____

State and Local Elections Comprehension Check

Directions: On a separate sheet of paper, answer the questions below according to the directions from your teacher.

★ Remember

List two offices at the state level. List two offices at the local level.

★ Understand

Explain why state and local elections are important.

★ Apply

You have just won the mayor's race. Draw a picture showing how you might spend your time in office. Write one or more sentences explaining what you are doing and why you are doing it.

★ Analyze

What if you wanted to run for mayor or governor? Write about what you would include in a commercial to explain what you would do in this office.

★ Evaluate

List five elected offices at the state or local levels. Rate these offices in order of importance. Explain your ratings.

★ Create

Who do you think would make a great governor or mayor? Create a campaign poster for the person you want to run for office.

Lesson 4: The Candidates

Standard

- Students know ways people can influence the decisions and actions of their government such as voting and taking an active role in political parties and other organizations that attempt to influence public policy and elections (McREL Civics 28.2)

Vocabulary

- ballot
- candidate
- politics
- run

Materials

- *The Candidates Content-Area Vocabulary* (page 52)
- *The Candidates Background Information* (page 53)
- *The Candidates Graphic Organizer* (page 54)
- *James K. Polk: Presidential Candidate Primary Source Connection* (pages 55–56)
- *Meet the Triangle Party Candidate* (page 57)
- *Meet the Square Party Candidate* (page 58)
- *The Candidates Comprehension Check* (page 59)

Introduce the Content

1. If you did not do the lesson titled *Political Parties* (page 16), then divide your class into two political parties at this time. One party is the Triangle Party. The other party is the Square Party. Allow students to name and create symbols for their parties.

2. Have students work with their political parties. Explain that they will meet their candidates soon. Have the Triangle Party think about ways candidates can help voters know who they are. Have the Square Party think about ways voters can get to know the candidates better. Have one spokesperson from each group share their ideas. List them on the board.

3. Distribute copies of *The Candidates Content Area Vocabulary* activity sheet (page 52) to students. Review the definitions as a class. Then, have students work with a partner to complete the activity. You may also ask students to complete one of the following Vocabulary Extension Activities.

✔ Vocabulary Extension Activities

- Ask students to explain how each term is related to a presidential election. Have them show the relationships on a separate sheet of paper.

- Tell students to pretend they are candidates who are "tossing their hats into the ring." Explain this idiom. Have students use each vocabulary term in a sentence related to this idea.

Lesson 4: The Candidates (cont.)

4. Explain that the process to run for president is more complicated than a person just announcing that he or she will run. Review the qualifications a person must have to run for president (see Lesson 2). Explain that a person must also be supported by his or her party. Distribute The Candidates Background Information activity sheet (page 53) and The Candidates Graphic Organizer (page 54) activity sheets to students. Read and discuss the information as a class or in small groups. Review how candidates might help voters know who they are, and how voters might get to know candidates better. Then allow students to complete the activity sheet independently or with their group.

Differentiation Idea

On sentence strips, list the steps that candidates take to help voters know them better, and the steps voters take to get to know candidates better. Meet with **below-level students** and **English language learners** in a small group to review the background information. Have students sort the sentence strips under two categories: Candidates Do This and Voters Do This.

5. Distribute copies of the James K. Polk: Presidential Candidate Primary Source Connection activity sheets (pages 55–56) to students. Discuss the photograph and information with the class. Then, allow students to complete the activity sheet with partners.

2 Day Conduct and Assess

1. Review the responsibilities of candidates and voters. Have students discuss the concept of politics.

2. Explain that students will meet their candidates now. Divide the class into their political groups. Have each group decide on one spokesperson. Distribute the appropriate Meet [My] Candidate activity sheet (page 57 or 58) to the spokesperson in each party. Read the directions as a class. Then, have the groups read about their candidate and record their ideas. Explain that the ideas they record will become part of the candidate's campaign in the next lesson.

3. Collect the groups' work for use during the next lesson.

4. Distribute copies of The Candidates Comprehension Check activity sheet (page 59) to assess students' understanding of candidates. Use the Comprehension Check Evaluation Rubric (page 15) to evaluate students' work. For further comprehension, have students complete the Research Extension (page 51) for homework.

Lesson 4: The Candidates (cont.)

Extension Ideas

☑ Find Out More

Research to find out which presidential election had the most candidates and which had the fewest candidates. Report your findings in the form of a graph.

☑ Research Extension

Have students research posters, advertisements, speeches, and public appearances that past presidents have given when they were candidates for president. Have students write the topics of the speeches or summarize the posters. They can share this information with their political party as they begin to prepare for the campaign.

☑ Connecting Elections

Students meet new people all the time. Some of these people may become good friends. But everyone must get to know each other better first. Have students think about a time when they met someone new. It might be a coach, a new student at school, or a distant cousin. Ask them to write a story to tell about how they got to know this person better.

Name: _____ Date: _____

The Candidates Content-Area Vocabulary

Directions: Look at the terms below. Write a definition for each vocabulary term in your own words. Then, write or draw an example for each term.

> **ballot**—a sheet of paper used to cast a vote
>
> **candidate**—a person running for political office
>
> **politics**—the act of being involved in government
>
> **run**—to compete in a race for political office

Vocabulary Term	Definition	Example
ballot		
candidate		
politics		
run		

Name: _____ Date: _____

The Candidates Background Information

Many people dream of being the next president or the next governor. Running for office takes a lot of dedication and hard work. First, people who want to run for public office must qualify for that race. They must check to be sure they can **run** for office. Then, they must be sure important people in **politics** know who they are. They attend meetings. They smile and speak a lot. They also shake hands with people. Finally, they get on the **ballot**. Each office has different steps to follow to do this. But, it is always important to make their name well known.

The people who want to be elected to public office are **candidates**. Candidates also need voters to know who they are. They want voters to know about their ideas. They hope the voters agree with their ideas. Then, the voters will probably vote for them!

Some candidates get on the ballot without a lot of name recognition. This means that not very many people know who they are. They must work extra hard to make sure the voters know their names by Election Day.

The candidates work to be sure you know who they are. They might appear on television ads or radio shows. Voters can hear about their ideas. Voters can hear how they might solve problems.

You might see their names and faces on billboards or signs. But, it is not all up to the candidates. Voters can learn more about the candidates by getting involved. Voters can become part of a political party. They can help with elections. They can attend meetings to hear the candidates speak. They can be part of another group that needs politicians. Say you want to help homeless animals. Your area might have a group that works to help find homes for homeless animals. But, this group needs help. They need support. Politicians can give this group the support it needs. So, the group leader might ask a candidate for help. In exchange, the group leader promises to support the candidate and vote for him or her. This is politics. People make promises to help each other. The candidate promises to help the group, and the group leader promises to support the candidate.

Voters have a very important responsibility when they vote. They vote for people who they believe will lead the government well. It is important that they know who their candidates are. They should know which candidates they agree with. They should know which candidates they believe will do the best job. Then, they can help the government become better.

Name: _____ Date: _____

The Candidates Graphic Organizer

Directions: Use the information from *The Candidates Background Information* activity sheet to explain each person's part during an election.

To help the voters know them, the candidates do these things:

- _____
  _____
- _____
  _____
- _____
  _____

To help themselves know the candidates better, voters can do these things:

- _____
  _____
- _____
  _____
- _____
  _____

1. Why is it important for voters to get to know the candidates before they vote?

_____

_____

2. Why do you think candidates need the support of other people in politics?

_____

_____

Name: _____ Date: _____

James K. Polk: Presidential Candidate Primary Source Connection

Directions: Read the information below.

Primary Source Background Information

This picture is printed. It is hand colored. It shows James K. Polk in 1844. He is "The People's Candidate for President," according to the print. Polk served as president from 1845 to 1849.

James K. Polk: Presidential Candidate
Primary Source Connection *(cont.)*
Primary Source Questions

Directions: Look at the James K. Polk picture. Then answer the questions below.

1. Describe what you see in the picture.

_____

_____

2. How is this print similar to and different from posters you might see of candidates today?

_____

_____

_____

3. The picture claims that Polk is "The People's Candidate." Do you think this was an effective slogan? Explain your thinking.

_____

_____

4. When this print was made, there was no television or Internet. There were no airplanes! What do you think James K. Polk did in 1844 to help voters know who he was?

_____

_____

_____

Primary Source Extension

Find out about James K. Polk's presidency. First, whom did he run against in 1844? From what you find out about him, why do you think he won the election? List three or more accomplishments of Polk's while he was in office. On a separate sheet of paper, explain why these were important.

Name: _____ Date: _____

Meet the Triangle Party Candidate

Directions: You belong to the Triangle Party. You believe you have a strong candidate. This person will run for president. Read about your candidate below. Write ideas about how the candidate can get voters to know more about her. Write ideas about how voters can get to know the candidate better.

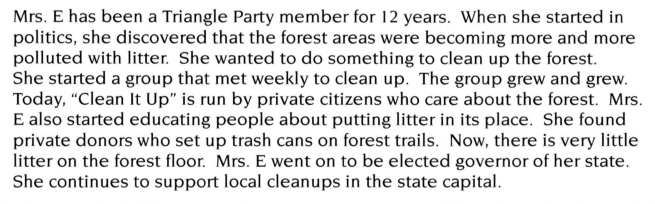

Triangle Party Candidate:

Mrs. E

Characteristics:

sly, smart, quick thinker

Political History:

Mrs. E has been a Triangle Party member for 12 years. When she started in politics, she discovered that the forest areas were becoming more and more polluted with litter. She wanted to do something to clean up the forest. She started a group that met weekly to clean up. The group grew and grew. Today, "Clean It Up" is run by private citizens who care about the forest. Mrs. E also started educating people about putting litter in its place. She found private donors who set up trash cans on forest trails. Now, there is very little litter on the forest floor. Mrs. E went on to be elected governor of her state. She continues to support local cleanups in the state capital.

To help voters know her better, Mrs. E can:	To get to know Mrs. E better, voters can:

Name: _____ Date: _____

Meet the Square Party Candidate

Directions: You belong to the Square Party. You believe you have a strong candidate. This person will run for president. Read about your candidate below. Write ideas about how the candidate can get voters to know more about him. Write ideas about how voters can get to know the candidate better.

Square Party Candidate:

Mr. J

Characteristics:

flexible, takes advantage of opportunities, hard worker

Political History:

Mr. J has been a Square Party member for ten years. His parents were Square Party officials. His grandparents were Square Party politicians, too. Mr. J was concerned about the growing amount of trash around wetland areas. He thought littering should be illegal. He wanted the government to pass tougher anti littering laws. He met with other Square Party politicians in the state capital. The government started a new group. It was the State Litter Control Board. Mr. J led this new group. He helped the government pass the first tough anti litter law. Many more laws followed. Mr. J still leads the State Litter Control Board. He is in charge of making sure that litter laws are followed and that litter cleanup crews do their jobs.

To help voters know him better, Mr. J can:	To get to know Mr. J better, voters can:

Name: _____ Date: _____

The Candidates Comprehension Check

Directions: On a separate sheet of paper, answer the questions below according to the directions from your teacher.

★ Remember

List two ways candidates can help voters get to know them better. List two ways voters can get to know candidates better.

★ Understand

Why do candidates want voters to get to know them? Explain why this is so important to candidates.

★ Apply

List three ways you could get to know a person better. Explain how each of these ideas will help you get to know this person better.

★ Analyze

Say you want to get to know a candidate better. Make a questionnaire for this person to complete. A questionnaire asks questions that help others find out about a person. Your questionnaire should have at least five questions.

★ Evaluate

Candidates need to get voters to know them better. What do you think are the best ways for candidates to get voters to know them better? List two of the best ideas, and explain why you think they are the best.

★ Create

Some politicians write books about their life's work. Make a book jacket for a fictional presidential candidate. Include a title, an author, and a publisher on the front. Include a short biography on the back. On the inside front cover, write a summary to explain how this person helped voters get to know him or her better. On the inside back cover, include a picture and explain what this person is doing now.

Lesson 5: On the Campaign Trail

Standard

- Students know ways people can influence the decisions and actions of their government such as voting; taking an active role in interest groups, political parties, and other organizations that attempt to influence public policy and elections; attending meetings of governing agencies; and working on campaigns (McREL Civics 28.2)

Vocabulary

- campaign
- debate
- issue
- media
- represent
- strategy

Materials

- *On the Campaign Trail Content-Area Vocabulary* (page 64)
- *On the Campaign Trail Background Information* (page 65)
- *On the Campaign Trail Graphic Organizer* (page 66)
- *Campaign Craze Primary Source Connection* (pages 67–68)
- *My Triangle Party Candidate's Campaign* (page 69)
- *My Square Party Candidate's Campaign* (page 70)
- *Campaign Contribution List* (page 71)
- *On the Campaign Trail Comprehension Check* (page 72)
- Examples of campaign posters or signs (*optional*)

Teacher Note: The *Campaign Contribution List* (page 71) has a sample list of production supplies students can use to develop their campaign advertisements. If needed, modify this list before making copies for the students to match the supplies students will have available to them. Gather these materials before the start of Day 2.

 ## Introduce the Content

1. If students did not participate in the previous lessons, discuss political parties with them. Then, divide the class into two political parties.

2. Review the responsibilities of both candidates and voters during an election year. Write the word *campaign* on the board. Ask students to brainstorm what they think this word means. List their ideas. Explain that there are many ways a candidate can campaign. They will have a chance to organize a campaign for their candidate.

3. Distribute copies of the *On the Campaign Trail Content-Area Vocabulary* activity sheet (page 64) to students. Read the terms and definitions together. Allow students to complete this activity sheet with a partner. You may also ask students to complete one of the following Vocabulary Extension Activities.

Lesson 5: On the Campaign Trail (cont.)

✔ Vocabulary Extension Activities

- Tell students to pretend they are newspaper reporters. What questions might they ask candidates running in a political race? Have them each write a list of three questions using the vocabulary words.

- As a class, create a campaign trail scrapbook. Students can bring in real-life or printed examples from current and past elections (e.g., buttons, bumper stickers, photos). In addition to the object, they must also explain when and how this particular item was used during the campaign.

4. Distribute copies of the On the Campaign Trail Background Information (page 65) and On the Campaign Trail Graphic Organizer (page 66). Read and discuss the information as a class. Discuss new information students learned about campaigns. Read the directions on the graphic organizer to students and allow them to work independently or with a partner to complete this activity sheet.

Differentiation Idea

Have **below-level** students and **English language learners** use highlighters to highlight details related to each term listed in the graphic organizer. Meet with them in a small group. Discuss the different types of campaign strategies. Work as a small group to complete the graphic organizer and encourage students to use their highlighted notes. Have **above-level** students explain their findings on a separate sheet of paper.

5. Distribute copies of the Campaign Craze Primary Source Connection activity sheet (pages 67–68) to students. Read the background information aloud. Discuss the questions as a class. Then, have students record their responses. For further comprehension, have students complete the primary source extension activity.

Begin the Activity

1. Begin this day by asking students to list different campaign strategies. Discuss which they believe would be the most effective, and why.

2. If possible, display examples of current or past political signs, posters, and television ads. Discuss the message of each strategy. Decide whether each particular strategy was effective, and explain why.

3. Divide the class into their political parties. Distribute copies of the appropriate My Party Candidate's Campaign (page 69 or 70) activity sheet to the spokesperson in each party. Read the directions as a class. Have the groups work collaboratively to fill in the blanks. They should use information they learned in Lesson 1 about political parties to do this.

 # Lesson 5: On the Campaign Trail *(cont.)*

4. Tell students that they should create a campaign strategy to highlight the good points about their candidate. They can keep notes in the center column, or on additional notebook paper. The spokesperson should lead the group to decide who will do what. Everyone in the group should have an assignment related to the campaign.

Differentiation Idea

Work with the groups to assign **below-level** students and **English language learners** campaign strategy tasks that are in line with their abilities and readiness levels.

5. Once students have adequately planned their campaign strategies, provide the needed materials for them to create their posters, banners, buttons, and other products. The *Campaign Contribution List* (page 71) may help students as they develop their ideas.

6. Collect and store the students' campaign materials to redistribute on Day 3. For an extension, have students bring in news clippings related to a current or past candidate. They should summarize the article and explain how the media played a role in this candidate's campaign.

Conclude and Assess

Day 3

1. Divide students into their political parties. Redistribute the needed campaign materials to students.

2. Allow students to use the class period finishing and displaying their posters, distributing buttons, or otherwise advertising their candidate.

3. Leave adequate class time for students to play their radio or television advertisements for the class.

4. Discuss how this experience has helped students understand more about political candidates' campaigns. Ask what they believe are the most effective campaign strategies and why they think this.

Teacher Note: If desired, assign dollar amounts to the items on the *Campaign Contribution List*. For example, each sheet of plain paper might be worth $1.25 while each sheet of colored paper might be worth $1.55. Have each party total how much of each item they used, and then sum up their campaign expenses. Discuss whether the students think candidates who spend more have a stronger campaign and why they think this.

5. Distribute copies of the *On the Campaign Trail Comprehension Check* activity sheet (page 72) to assess students' understanding of campaigns. Use the Comprehension Check Evaluation Rubric (page 15) to evaluate students' work.

 # Lesson 5: On the Campaign Trail *(cont.)*

Extension Ideas

☑ Find Out More

Tell students that the elections office and their local party headquarters are good places to find out more about political campaigns. They could call or visit to find out the answers to questions such as:

- Is there a limit on the number of signs a candidate can post?

- Are there guidelines to tell where a candidate may and may not display signs?

- Who sets up political events, such as speeches and debates? Where are they usually held? How are they advertised so that the public knows about them?

Another option is to invite leaders from both local party headquarters, or from your local supervisor of elections to answer the class's questions related to campaigning.

☑ Research Extension

Campaigns cost candidates a lot of money. Have students find out how much candidates from past races have spent on their campaigns. They should also investigate where most of this money comes from.

☑ Connecting Elections

Have students think about advertising they have seen for toys or candy. These advertisements might be on signs in the store, on billboards, on television, or the radio. Have students work in small groups to talk about how this kind of advertising compares to a candidate's campaign. They should think about successful toy and candy advertisements, and how candidates can apply these advertising techniques to their own campaign.

Name: _____ Date: _____

On the Campaign Trail Content-Area Vocabulary

Directions: The terms below all have something to do with campaigns. Read the definitions. Read the descriptions. List the terms with their descriptions. Finish the sentences. Use each term only one time.

---

campaign—an organized effort to achieve a specific goal, like getting elected

debate—a discussion between two or more people in which ideas are given for or against issues

issue—a matter for discussion or debate; a public concern

media—a way to report, write, edit, photograph, or otherwise show the news

represent—to stand in for; act for; be a symbol for

strategy—a plan of action

Description	Term
This might include speeches, posters, and television ads.	1.
The bald eagle does this for America.	2.
Television, radio, and Internet are all examples of this.	3.
Football coaches plan this to help their team win the game.	4.
The economy, taxes, and health care are popular ones of these.	5.
Sometimes these can get heated. This means people get upset. They might start shouting. Many times, they are calm. People take sides.	6.

Name: _____ Date: _____

On the Campaign Trail Background Information

A candidate has decided to run for public office. He or she is eligible to run for this office. He or she has qualified to run. Now, the real work begins. The candidate must get his or her message to voters. The candidate must convince everyone that he or she is the best candidate for the job! The candidate starts his or her **campaign**. This is how the candidate helps voters get to know him or her better.

There are two main political parties. They are Democrats and Republicans. On Election Day, only one candidate will **represent** each party. Voters will have a clear choice. But, many people from the same party may want to run for this office. So, there is a primary election. This happens before Election Day. Voters choose the person from each party they want to see on the Election Day ballot.

All the candidates campaign all the way up to the primary election. They may all have different campaign **strategies**. But they have some things in common. They will put their messages and faces on billboards. They will put their names and slogans on signs. They will advertise on the radio and on television. They will speak about important **issues**. The public comes to these speeches. They hear first hand from the candidates. Sometimes there is a **debate**. This is where candidates strongly state their positions about the issues. They try to convince voters that their ideas are better than the ideas of their opponents.

Primary elections usually take place in February before the November election. This means that candidates must campaign hard and fast to sway voters in their favor. By the time the primaries come, voters have heard the messages. They have made their decision. They cast their vote. The winner for each party is chosen at a convention or caucus in the summer. Here, the campaign ends for some. But for the winners of each party, the campaign continues. They have just a few months left to work on getting voters excited about them. The **media** covers a lot of campaign events leading up to the election. They report about these events on the news. This helps voters stay informed. Candidates will give hundreds of speeches. They will take part in many interviews. They will debate the issues with one another. Their job is to make voters want them in that office. They want as many votes as possible so they will win the election in November!

Name: _____ Date: _____

On the Campaign Trail Graphic Organizer

Directions: All these things are part of running a campaign. Use details from the *On the Campaign Trail Background Information* activity sheet to explain in the middle box how each item is part of a campaign. Illustrate each idea in the bottom box.

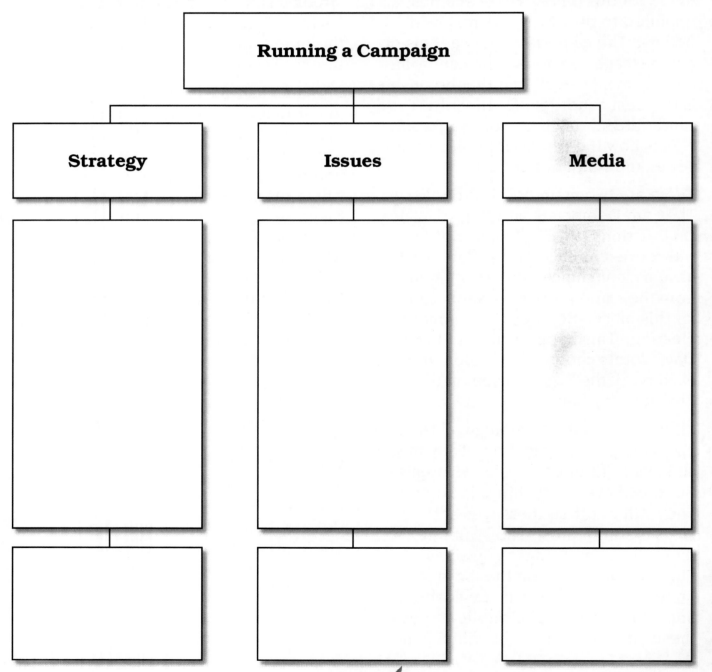

Name: _____ Date: _____

Campaign Craze Primary Source Connection

Directions: Read the information below.

Primary Source Background Information

This picture shows political campaign signs lining the walkway leading up to an election precinct. A precinct is a voting site. These signs were displayed by candidates running for public office during the 2010 election. This voting site was at Hine Junior High School in Washington, DC.

Name: _____ Date: _____

Campaign Craze Primary Source Connection *(cont.)*

Primary Source Questions

Directions: Look at the picture. Then answer the questions below.

1. What does the picture show?

_____

_____

2. How many different candidates' signs can you count?

_____

3. What on the signs grabs your attention or stands out to you?

_____

_____

4. Do you think these campaign signs made a difference for the candidates? Explain your thinking.

_____

_____

_____

5. If you were a voter going to this precinct, how would the signs affect your vote?

_____

_____

_____

Primary Source Extension

If it is an election year, keep track of the campaign signs and billboards you see on the road, around town, and in your neighborhood. Keep a log to record:

- Who the signs are for
- Which race they are running in

- Any colors, letter styles, or other characteristics that stand out to you
- When the signs seem to become very numerous

Name: _____ Date: _____

My Triangle Party Candidate's Campaign

Directions: Your candidate wants to run for president! List three or more words to describe your candidate. List two other ideas your candidate believes in.

My Candidate's Name: Mrs. E

My Candidate is a member of the Triangle Party.

Words to describe my candidate:

_____ _____ _____

_____ _____ _____

My candidate believes in:

_____ small government _____ _____ fewer laws to keep people safe _____

_____ care with money _____ _____ personal responsibility _____

_____ _____

Campaign Strategies

Directions: Create a campaign strategy for Mrs. E. List details about each strategy. Name the person in your group who will be responsible for each strategy. Then, use the materials provided by your teacher to create posters, buttons, banners, and advertisements to promote your candidate.

Strategy	Notes	Person(s) Responsible
slogan		
posters and signs		
television and radio ads		
speeches and appearances		

Name: _____ Date: _____

My Square Party Candidate's Campaign

Directions: Your candidate wants to run for president! List three or more words to describe your candidate. List two other ideas your candidate believes in.

My Candidate's Name: Mr. J

My Candidate is a member of the Square Party.

Words to describe my candidate:

_____ _____ _____

_____ _____ _____

My candidate believes in:

big government	many laws to keep people safe
political power	health care for everyone

Campaign Strategies

Directions: Create a campaign strategy for Mr. J. List details about each strategy. Name the person in your group who will be responsible for each strategy. Then, use the materials provided by your teacher to create posters, buttons, banners, and advertisements to promote your candidate.

Strategy	Notes	Person(s) Responsible
slogan		
posters and signs		
television and radio ads		
speeches and appearances		

Name: _____ Date: _____

Campaign Contribution List

Directions: The things listed below will help you create your campaign advertisements. Check the box for each item you will need or create your own. Give it to your teacher along with your plan.

❏ blank paper   ❏ safety pins

❏ colored paper   ❏ use of video camera

❏ construction paper   ❏ tape recorder

❏ poster paper   ❏ audio tapes

❏ butcher paper   ❏ computer

❏ streamers   ❏ black and white printer

❏ balloons   ❏ color printer

❏ magic markers   ❏ poster printer

❏ glue   _____

❏ scissors   _____

❏ scotch tape   _____

❏ masking tape   _____

Name: _____ Date: _____

On the Campaign Trail Comprehension Check

Directions: On a separate sheet of paper, answer the questions below according to the directions from your teacher.

★ Remember

List three ways candidates can campaign.

★ Understand

Explain how the media plays a part in a candidate's campaign.

★ Apply

Pretend that you are a voter. Describe three kinds of advertisements you have seen from the candidates running for office.

★ Analyze

In a complete paragraph, explain why campaign strategies are important.

★ Evaluate

Which type of campaign strategy do you think is the most effective? Explain why you think this.

★ Create

Develop a campaign strategy for a presidential candidate. Design a poster, sign, or billboard for a fictional candidate. Create a slogan for this fictional candidate. Write a 15 to 30 second radio advertisement for this candidate.

Lesson 6: Making a Difference

Standard

- Students know ways people can influence the decisions and actions of their government such as voting; taking an active role in interest groups, political parties, and other organizations that attempt to influence public policy and elections; attending meetings of governing agencies; circulating and signing petitions; taking part in peaceful demonstrations; and contributing money to political parties, candidates, or causes (McREL Civics 28.2)

Vocabulary

- demonstration
- forum
- influence
- interest group
- petition
- rally

Materials

- *Making a Difference Content-Area Vocabulary* (page 77)
- *Making a Difference Background Information* (page 78)
- Making a *Difference Graphic Organizer* (page 79)
- *Farmers' Rally Primary Source Connection* (pages 80–81)
- *Join the Triangle Party Rally* (page 82)
- *Join the Square Party Rally* (page 83)
- *Making a Difference Comprehension Check* (page 84)
- Art supplies (e.g., markers, glue, scissors)

Introduce the Content

1. If students did not participate in the previous lessons, discuss political parties with them. Then, divide the class into two political parties.

2. Explain that ordinary citizens can influence politicians to make decisions in government. Have students discuss with a partner about how this might be accomplished. Then, have volunteers share their ideas.

3. Distribute copies of the *Making a Difference Content-Area Vocabulary* activity sheet (page 77) to students. Review the definitions as a class. Allow students to work in small groups or with a partner to complete the activity sheet. Have volunteers share their additional examples and nonexamples for each term with the class. You may also ask students to complete one of the following Vocabulary Extension Activities.

 # Lesson 6: Making a Difference *(cont.)*

☑ Vocabulary Extension Activities

- Have students work with a partner to write original sentences with the terms.

- Have students choose two vocabulary terms. Then, ask them to compare and contrast those terms on Venn diagrams. Allow students to share their Venn diagrams in small groups so that others may be further exposed to the terms that they did not choose.

4. Distribute copies of the *Making a Difference Background Information* (page 78) and the *Making a Difference Graphic Organizer* (page 79) activity sheets to students. Divide the class into small groups. Have students read the information in their groups and complete the graphic organizer.

Differentiation Ideas

- Place **English language learners** with students who can help them as they read and answer the questions. These students should have complete understanding of the questions and vocabulary so that they can help explain it to the English language learners.

- Consider writing some details on the organizer before copying the graphic organizer for **below-level** students and **English language learners**. This will reduce their workload to only reading and recording the who, what, where, and when questions.

5. Distribute copies of the *Farmers' Rally Primary Source Connection* activity sheet (pages 80–81) to students. Discuss the picture with students. Then, ask them to complete the questions concerning the pictures. Students who do not finish their primary source sheets in class can do so as homework.

 ## Begin the Activity

1. Begin this day by reviewing ways ordinary citizens can get involved in influencing government decisions and policies.

Extension Idea

Find Out More

Have students watch footage of Dr. Martin Luther King Jr.'s "I Have a Dream" speech. Discuss the impact of this political rally and the influence his speech had with regard to laws, government, and politics.

2. Collect students' completed primary source sheets. Discuss students' answers to the primary source questions.

3. Explain to students that it is now time to plan a rally for an interest group that wants its party candidate's support. Divide students into their political parties.

Lesson 6: Making a Difference *(cont.)*

4. Explain to students that a rally is one way a special interest group can gain attention to an issue that is important to them. Have students work with a partner to discuss the difference between a rally and a demonstration. Have students share their ideas with the class. Explain that during a demonstration, people usually demand action with regard to the issue. During a rally, people generally drum up support and get people excited about the issues being addressed.

5. Distribute the appropriate *Join the Party Rally* activity sheet (page 82 or 83) to the spokesperson in each political group. Read the directions as a class. Then, as a group, students should plan their rally. Explain that every student should be assigned a role. Provide the necessary art supplies for them to plan and prepare for their rally.

Differentiation Idea

Allow students at **all levels** to choose which tasks they would like to plan for the rally. This way, they can choose the areas that will magnify their strengths.

Conclude and Assess

1. Today is Rally Day! Allow students to display any posters or signs. Set up two areas in the room for speeches and entertainment. Have each party take turns with each event. All students will listen and watch during each event. As the teacher, rate each party's rally with regard to how influential it was. Use this rating scale:

   5—extremely influential
   4—very influential
   3—somewhat influential
   2—slightly influential
   1—not influential

2. At the conclusion of the rally, inform the class of the most influential rally. If it is the Triangle Party, explain that Mrs. E will provide incentives for private organizations to sponsor child-centered events (e.g., roller skating, bowling, biking). She will also work with government agencies that already exist (e.g., police and fire departments, local libraries). If it is the Square Party, explain that Mr. J will start a new government agency, funded with tax dollars, to create fun activities for kids at local parks and public facilities (e.g., community pool, public library). He will put this agency in charge of making sure the activities occur, requiring a certain number of hours each week for student-centered activities.

Lesson 6: Making a Difference (cont.)

3. Discuss how the support of this candidate might influence voter decisions when they go to vote. Discuss how the outcome may have differed had the class had a demonstration or forum (debate) with regard to this issue, or if their party had simply circulated a petition.

4. Assess students' understanding of citizen involvement in government by having them complete the *Making a Difference Comprehension Check* activity sheet (page 84). Use the Comprehension Check Evaluation Rubric (page 15) to evaluate students' work.

Extension Ideas

✔ Find Out More

Rallies and demonstrations can have a powerful impact when conducted in large cities, state capitals, and the nation's capital. However, some small communities also hold demonstrations and rallies. Have students go online to their local newspaper to research past and upcoming events such as political rallies and demonstrations that have occurred near them.

✔ Research Extension

Not all politicians follow through with their promises. Have students research a presidential candidate's campaign, including his position with regard to public issues. They should find out what his campaign promises were, and whether he saw them through during his presidency.

✔ Connecting Elections

Persuading people to see their side of an issue can sometimes be challenging. Have students think about a time when they had to persuade someone to do something or think a certain way, or about a time when they were the person being persuaded. Have them write a personal account of this situation, including whether the person could be persuaded.

Name: _____ Date: _____

Making a Difference Content-Area Vocabulary

Directions: Read these examples and nonexamples for each vocabulary term. Decide which term the examples and nonexamples describe. Use the definitions to help you. Write the word in the space. Add one more example and one more nonexample for each word.

> **demonstration**—an organized protest by a group of people
>
> **forum**—a meeting where people openly discuss and debate issues
>
> **influence**—to persuade or sway someone to think or act differently
>
> **interest group**—a group of people who agree about a certain issue
>
> **petition**—a written paper asking for a change
>
> **rally**—an organized assembly where people build enthusiasm for a cause

Examples	Term	Nonexamples
The Sierra Club National Organization for Women _____		Boy Scouts chorus _____
sit-in picket with signs _____		picnic fishing _____
paper request signature page _____		permission slip driver's license _____
debate discussion _____		movie book club _____
persuade convince _____		argue disagree _____
pep anti-war _____		barbecue pool party _____

Name: _____ Date: _____

Making a Difference Background Information

People become candidates in political races because they want to make a difference. They want to take part in government. Not everyone is interested in becoming a politician. Some people cannot run for public office, even if they want to. Still, there are many ways citizens can get involved in government. They can make a difference, even if they are not elected to public office.

The most important way citizens can make a difference is to vote. But an election seems far off after the primary elections. There is a lot going on during an election year. After all, the election is not until November! People can get involved long before Election Day. One way they can do this is to help with a candidate's campaign. Maybe they know someone who is running. Maybe they just have a favorite candidate. They can volunteer to put signs up around the community. They can help with **rallies** and **forums**. They can call the newspaper to let them know about these events. Or, they can simply donate money.

Also, citizens can join clubs that help support the candidates. An **interest group** is one kind of club. This is a group of people who have a common goal. They act together to achieve their goal. Your school may have a Parent-Teacher Association (PTA). This is an interest group. Their goal is to support the school. Political interest groups get together to try to change laws. They work to make the government better. Local political parties also have clubs.

These clubs have meetings. They talk about how their involvement supports the community.

Some laws need the help of voters. Politicians can sometimes be persuaded to act when many people join together. One way this is done is through a **petition**. Citizens can pass around petitions. They ask other people to sign them. Some petitions get many, many signatures. Candidates may use the issue on the petition to help them win over voters. Another way to persuade politicians is through a **demonstration**. This is when a lot of people get together in one place and do the same thing. They may wave signs. They may sit still for many days. They may march down a city street. They want politicians to pay attention to them. They have a message. They want to be heard.

Some people have no time to volunteer. Still, there are speeches and debates to hear. These are open to the public. The candidates want people to come! Here, voters can hear about what the candidates have to say on the issues. After the election, people can stay involved. They can attend city council meetings. They can attend school board meetings. They can hear what is going on. They can speak at these meetings. This makes their voice heard, too. There are many ways people can **influence** the government.

Name: _____ Date: _____

Making a Difference Graphic Organizer

Directions: Use the information from the *Making a Difference Background Information* activity sheet to write details in the wheel about how citizens can influence the government.

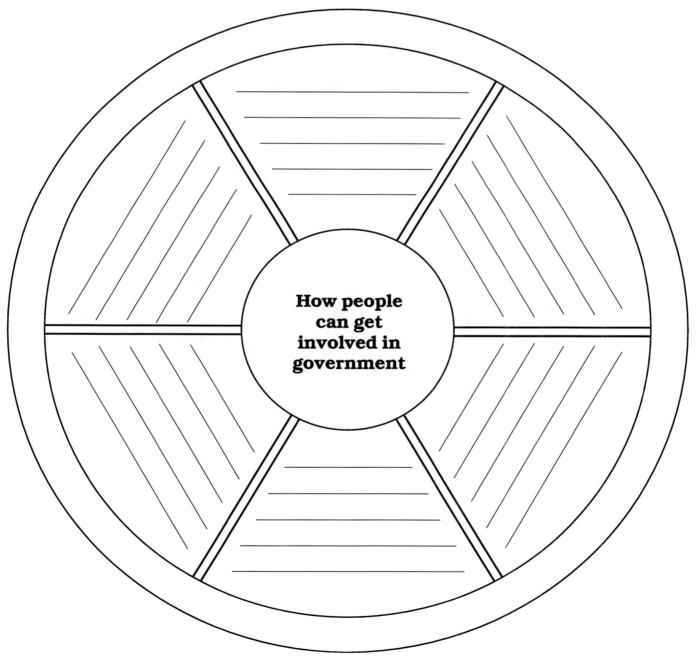

How people
can get
involved in
government

Name: _____ Date: _____

Farmers' Rally Primary Source Connection

Directions: Read the information below.

Primary Source Background Information

This picture is from 1977. Farmers drove their tractors right into downtown Washington, DC! They held a nighttime rally. This was the start of the American Agriculture Movement (AAM). Farmers were worried about the prices they were paid for their crops. They were concerned for their families. They were concerned for the nation. Notice the sign in the front. A strike is when people refuse to work in order to gain higher pay. This was the first time farmers took a stand. The media helped spread their message. The AAM is still strong today. They act to keep politicians thinking about farmers and the work they do.

Farmers' Rally Primary Source Connection *(cont.)*

Primary Source Questions

Directions: Use the information from the *Farmers' Rally Primary Source Connection* activity sheet. Think about the picture. Answer the questions below.

1. What is this picture mostly about?

_____

_____

2. This was a new experience for most farmers. Some of them had never left home. Describe how they might have felt entering Washington, DC for the first time.

_____

_____

3. What role do you think the media played in spreading the farmers' message?

_____

_____

_____

4. Do you think this was a successful rally? Explain your thinking.

_____

_____

_____

Primary Source Extension

Find out about other public rallies and demonstrations that have affected government decisions. Explain who the special interest group is, why they rallied, and whether their efforts were successful. Create a poster to share this information with the class.

Name: _____ Date: _____

Join the Triangle Party Rally

Directions: Work with your political group. The Triangle Party candidate, Mrs. E, might be influenced to change events and activities for kids. Plan and have a rally to encourage others to join your interest in this issue.

Issue: There are not enough events and activities for kids living in your area.

Special Interest Group: Citizens for Increased Activities (CIA)

Rally Date: _____   **Time:** _____

Rally Location: _____

Rally Events:

1. three speeches from concerned CIA members

2. chants and cheers from CIA party members

3. food (specify) _____

4. entertainment (specify) _____

5. entertainment (specify) _____

How will you advertise this rally to get public support?

_____

_____

_____

How will these events influence Mrs. E? What do you want her to do?

_____

_____

Rally Extension: Write a newspaper article to inform the public about this rally. Explain who was involved, where it took place, when it took place, what CIA is, why it took place, and how CIA wants action from Mrs. E.

Name: _____ Date: _____

Join the Square Party Rally

Directions: Work with your political group. The Square Party candidate, Mr. J, might be influenced to change events and activities for kids. Plan and have a rally to encourage others to join your interest in this issue.

Issue: There are not enough events and activities for kids living in your area.

Special Interest Group: Kids Demanding Fun (KDF)

Rally Date: _____ **Time:** _____

Rally Location: _____

Rally Events:

1. three speeches from concerned KDF members

2. chants and cheers from KDF party members

3. food (specify) _____

4. entertainment (specify) _____

5. entertainment (specify) _____

How will you advertise this rally to get public support?

_____

_____

_____

How will these events influence Mr. J? What do you want him to do?

_____

_____

Rally Extension: Write a newspaper article to inform the public about this rally. Explain who was involved, where it took place, when it took place, what KDF is, why it took place, and how KDF wants action from Mr. J.

Name: _____ Date: _____

Making a Difference Comprehension Check

Directions: On a separate sheet of paper, answer the questions below according to the directions from your teacher.

★ Remember

List three or more ways citizens can help influence the government, even when they are not running for office.

★ Understand

Write a paragraph. Explain what a rally is. Explain who organizes it and why it takes place.

★ Apply

You are part of the Support for Lost Animals special interest group. Create a scrapbook of the events where you will have to make your interests known to others. Include three or more "pictures" with captions. Also include one newspaper article describing one event related to your interest.

★ Analyze

Compare a rally to a demonstration. Record your ideas in a Venn diagram.

★ Evaluate

Which of the following do you believe is the most influential way special interest groups can make their ideas known: demonstrations, rallies, forums, or petitions? Explain your thinking.

★ Create

Create a list of events for a rally. Include the date, location, and goals of the rally. List events and speakers in the order in which they will take place. Explain why you believe this rally will be successful.

 # Lesson 7: The History of Voting

Standard

- Students know that a citizen is a legally recognized member of the United States who has certain rights and privileges and certain responsibilities (McREL Civics 24.1)

Vocabulary

- amendment
- cast a vote
- citizen
- poll
- responsibility
- right

Materials

- *The History of Voting Content-Area Vocabulary* (page 88)
- *The History of Voting Background Information* (page 89)
- *The History of Voting Graphic Organizer* (page 90)
- *Women Voters Primary Source Connection* (pages 91–92)
- *The Rights and Responsibilities of Voting* (page 93)
- *The History of Voting Comprehension Check* (page 94)
- Art supplies (e.g., poster boards, construction paper, markers, glue, tape)

 ## Introduce the Content

1. If students did not participate in the previous lessons, discuss political parties with them. Then, divide the class into two political parties.

2. Write this statement on the board: *All American citizens can vote in elections.* Poll the class to find out how many students believe this statement is true, and how many believe it is false. Explain that it would be a true statement if it read, "All American citizens over the age of 18 can vote." Discuss the difference between the two statements.

3. Ask the class to think about the words *all American citizens.* Discuss the meaning of this phrase in today's context. Explain that at one time, *all citizens* did not mean "all citizens." Discuss how this might be true.

4. Distribute copies of *The History of Voting Content Area Vocabulary* activity sheet (page 88) activity sheet to students. Read the definitions as a class. Allow students to complete this page with a partner. You may also ask students to complete a Vocabulary Extension Activity.

 # Lesson 7: The History of Voting *(cont.)*

Vocabulary Extension Activities

- Ask students to pretend they are writers for newspapers. Their jobs are to find good quotes to use in articles concerning elections. Ask students to create three quotes that might be used in an article about elections. They should use one vocabulary term in each of their quotes.

- Have students make an acrostic poem for three or more vocabulary terms. Each sentence should have something to do with voting or elections.

5. Distribute copies of *The History of Voting Background Information* (page 89) and *The History of Voting Graphic Organizer* (page 90) activity sheets to students. Allow them to read the information with partners. When they finish reading, have each person ask two or three questions of his or her partner to answer using information from the text. Then, they can collaborate to complete the activity sheet.

Differentiation Idea

List the dates on the graphic organizer for **below-level** students and **English language learners.** Meet with them as a small group to review the information in the text, scanning for the dates. Reread these sections as a group and summarize the information in these paragraphs. Then, work with students to complete the rest of the graphic organizer.

6. Distribute copies of the *Women Voters Primary Source Connection* activity sheet (pages 91–92) to students. Discuss the picture as a class. Then, ask students to complete the questions in small groups within their political parties. Have a class discussion about the picture.

 ## Begin the Activity

1. Have students sit with their political parties. Discuss the idea of voting being both a right and a responsibility. Then, ask students whether they think every eligible citizen follows through with the right and responsibility of voting, and why this might be.

2. Distribute copies of *The Rights and Responsibilities of Voting* activity sheet (page 93) to students. Read and discuss the questions as a class. Also spend time reviewing and analyzing the data in the tables. Have students work with their political groups to list ideas to possibly explain why people do not vote, and ideas they have to increase voter turnout.

Differentiation Idea

As an extension, **above-level** students can create a graph representation of their findings from the activity sheet *The Rights and Responsibilities of Voting*.

 # Lesson 7: The History of Voting *(cont.)*

3. Have volunteers share with the class their reasons to explain why people do not vote. List their ideas on the board. Then, have students share their ideas to encourage greater voter turnout. List these ideas on the board as well.

4. Explain that students will have an opportunity to go to the polls during the next lesson. They want 100 percent voter turnout. So, they will collaborate to complete the tasks that will encourage voters to cast their vote on Election Day. Have students work together with their political parties to put their ideas into motion. Provide students with the necessary art supplies to complete their tasks.

Differentiation Idea

Meet with **English language learners** in a small group. Discuss the ideas listed to help increase voter turnout. Then, assign them tasks they can accomplish.

5. Allow students the remainder of class time to complete their tasks.

 # Conclude and Assess

1. Distribute the materials from Day 2, and allow students to display, post, or conduct their activities to hopefully increase voter turnout.

2. Discuss the effectiveness of the students' attempts to increase voter turnout.

3. Distribute copies of *The History of Voting Comprehension Check* activity sheet (page 94) to assess students' understanding of how people contribute to campaigns. Use the Comprehension Check Evaluation Rubric (page 15) to evaluate students' work.

Extension Ideas

Find Out More

Encourage students to contact their own supervisor of elections office to find out the voter turnout rates in their district(s) for the past decade. Have students present this information in graph form.

Research Extension

Have students interview their adult family members, adult friends, and close neighbors to find out how many did and did not vote in the most recent election, and whether they intend to vote in the upcoming election. For each response, students should also inquire why they do vote, and why they do not vote. Have students summarize their research for the class.

Connecting Elections

Some students may avoid personal responsibilities such as doing homework or cleaning their room. Have them complete a Venn diagram to compare any one responsibility with the responsibility of voting. They should justify which is a greater responsibility and why.

Name: _____ Date: _____

The History of Voting Content-Area Vocabulary

Directions: Read the terms and definitions below. Write each term in the correct sentence.

amendment—a law added to the Constitution
cast a vote—choose a candidate for office in an election
citizen—a member of a city, state, or nation
poll—a place where people go to vote
responsibility—something someone should do; a duty; an obligation
right—something someone is entitled to have or do

1. Kendra tried to tell Mya that she could not run for president of their youth club. But Mya insisted that it was her _____ to do so.

2. The election was the next day. The last message the candidate spoke to his supporters was, "See you at the _____ tomorrow!"

3. I know doing my homework is my _____. But sometimes I just do not feel like doing it.

4. The 15th _____ gave the right to vote to people of any race or color.

5. Every student in our school _____ for his or her favorite book. I cannot wait to see which title won the election!

6. Everyone should strive to be a good _____.

Name: _____ Date: _____

The History of Voting Background Information

Candidates running for public office want voters to choose them for the position. They hold events that voters will like. They say things that voters will like. Then, it is time for voters to go to the **polls**. They **cast their vote** for their favorite candidate.

Anyone over the age of 18 can vote. But, this was not always the case. The 26th **Amendment** to the Constitution changed the voting age. It used to be 21. After 1971, it was 18. It passed because soldiers went to fight in war at the age of 18. But, they were not old enough to vote! This seemed unfair. So, this amendment lowered the voting age.

An amendment is a change. New laws have been added to the Constitution after it was written. The first ten laws are called the Bill of Rights. They were added right away. Other laws were added as time went on.

Voting **rights** have changed many times since 1776. At first, only white landowners could vote. Then, amendments were added to the Constitution. Three of them changed voting rights for different people. One amendment is the 15th. It said that a person of any race or color could vote. It was added in 1870. This was right after the Civil War. Slaves had been freed. They were now allowed to vote. Another amendment is the 19th. It gave the right to vote to women. Women voted for the first time in 1920. They worked very hard to have the right to vote, just like men.

Today, all **citizens** of the United States over the age of 18 can vote. A citizen is a person who lives legally in the United States. People become citizens by being born here. If they are from other countries, they can take special classes. They take a special oath. Then, they can become United States citizens.

Voting is a legal right granted to citizens in the Constitution. Citizens can also hold public office. This is another right. Some laws set minimum age limits on public offices. Each office has its own rules related to who can run. But, it is a right for anyone who wants to do so. Voting is also a **responsibility**. This means that citizens who are eligible to vote should do so. It is their civic duty. It is the most important way citizens can affect laws and government. They cast their vote for the person who they think will do the best job.

Name: _____ Date: _____

The History of Voting Graphic Organizer

Directions: Use information from *The History of Voting Background Information* activity sheet. Write details about each amendment listed. Answer the questions below.

History of Voting	15th Amendment	19th Amendment	26th Amendment
Year			
Who It Affected			
How It Changed Voting Rights			

1. How many years have passed since the last voting amendment was added?

_____

2. Why do you think it took so long for voting rights to be granted to all citizens no matter their color, race, or gender?

_____

_____

3. Why is voting a right?

_____

_____

4. How is voting a responsibility?

_____

_____

Name: _____ Date: _____

Women Voters Primary Source Connection

Directions: Read the information below.

Primary Source Background Information

The women's suffrage movement lasted from 1870 to 1920. Suffrage was a time when women fought for their right to vote. They thought the 15th Amendment gave them this right. But many women were turned away at the polls. Before 1920, some states did allow women to vote in elections. In fact, Esther Morris was appointed as a judge in South Pass City, Wyoming, in 1870. She was the first female government official. This picture is from about 1817. It shows three suffragists casting their votes. These women appear calm and confident.

Name: _____ Date: _____

Women Voters Primary Source Connection (cont.)

Primary Source Questions

Directions: Look at the picture. Answer the questions below.

1. Why is this picture an important part of history?

_____

_____

2. Why would women have believed the 15th Amendment gave them the right to vote?

_____

_____

3. What happened in 1920 that brought women's suffrage to an end?

_____

_____

4. Do you believe the women are as calm and confident as they appear? Explain your answer.

_____

_____

_____

Primary Source Extension

Pretend you are a woman going to vote for the first time. Or, pretend you are a man at the polls when the first woman shows up to vote. On a separate sheet of paper, write a personal narrative describing the scene, and how you and those around you behave.

Name: _____ Date: _____

The Rights and Responsibilities of Voting

Directions: Read the information. Answer the questions below.

Voting is a legal right. All eligible citizens are allowed to vote.

Voting is a civic responsibility. All eligible citizens should vote in elections.

1. How is voting both a right and a responsibility? What is the difference?

_____

_____

Voter turnout can be low. This means that very few people who can vote do vote. Look at these voter turnout rates:

Voter Turnout 2008	
(Presidential Election)	
United States	61.6%
California	61.2%
Florida	66.9%
New York	58.3%
Texas	54.4%

Voter Turnout 2010	
(Non Presidential Election)	
United States	40.9%
California	44.1%
Florida	42.2%
New York	34.9%
Texas	32.3%

2. What conclusions can you draw from this data?

_____

_____

3. Why do you think people do not vote?

_____

_____

4. What ideas do you have to get more people to the polls?

_____

_____

Name: _____ Date: _____

The History of Voting Comprehension Check

Directions: On a separate sheet of paper, answer the questions below according to the directions from your teacher.

★ Remember

List the three constitutional amendments that changed voting laws. Also name which group of people each amendment directly affected.

★ Understand

Explain how voting is both a right and a responsibility.

★ Apply

Someone you know just told you that he or she does not plan to vote. Write a dialogue between you and this person. Write what you would say to this person, and how the person might respond.

★ Analyze

Explain why voter turnout rates tend to be lower during non presidential elections.

★ Evaluate

What are some challenges people may face on Election Day with regard to getting to the polls to cast their vote? What, if anything, can be done to help them overcome their challenges?

★ Create

Create a chant, cheer, or rap that encourages all eligible citizens to vote.

Lesson 8: Going to the Polls

Standard

- Students know qualities leaders should have such as commitment to the values and principles of constitutional democracy, respect for the rights of others, ability to work with others, reliability or dependability, courage, honesty, ability to be fair, intelligence, willingness to work hard, and special knowledge or skills (McREL Civics 29.5)

Vocabulary

- constitutional democracy
- Election Day
- trait
- value

Materials

- *Going to the Polls Content-Area Vocabulary* (page 99)
- *Going to the Polls Background Information* (page 100)
- *Going to the Polls* (page 101)
- *Taking the Oath of Office Primary Source Connection* (pages 102–103)
- *Candidate Values and Traits* (page 104)
- *Voter Application* (page 105)
- *Voter Identification Cards* (page 106)
- *Voting Ballots* (page 107)
- *Going to the Polls Comprehension Check* (page 108) (*optional*)
- Shoe box
- Wrapping paper or brown grocery bags

- Class list with lines after student names for signatures
- "I Voted" stickers (*optional*)

Introduce the Content

1. If students did not participate in the previous lessons, discuss political parties with them. Then, divide the class into two political parties.

2. Have students think about someone they know who they think would make a fantastic presidential candidate. Have them turn to a partner, share their nominee, and explain why they think this person would make a good president. Then, ask volunteers to share the person they named with the class along with the traits they exhibit. List the reasons why students mentioned this person on the board. Explain that voters have the responsibility of electing people to public office. Therefore, they want to be sure the people they vote for are quality candidates. Discuss the qualities listed on the board.

 # Lesson 8: Going to the Polls *(cont.)*

3. Distribute copies of the *Going to the Polls Content Area Vocabulary* activity sheet (page 99) to students. Review the definitions as a class. Then, allow students to complete this activity sheet with a partner. You may also ask students to complete one of the following Vocabulary Extension Activities.

✔ Vocabulary Extension Activities

- Have students create "Can You Name the Political Term?" games. Have students create flashcards that give clues for each vocabulary word. They should write the vocabulary words on the backs of the cards. Allow students to work with partners to see if they can name the vocabulary words using the clues created.

- Ask students to read newspaper articles or watch the news. Have them record how many examples of each vocabulary word are used in the news. Ask them to record the vocabulary words on paper and explain how each word was used in the media.

4. Tell students that they will soon be participating in the general election. Distribute copies of the *Going to the Polls Background Information* (page 100) and the *Going to the Polls* (page 101) activity sheets to students. Allow students to read the information with partners. Then, discuss the sheet as a whole class. Read the directions on the activity sheet together. Allow students to review the information from the background information sheet and complete the activity with their reading partner.

Differentiation Idea

Meet as a small group with **struggling students** and **English language learners**. Discuss the information from the text. Have students find and circle the words *value* and *trait*. Give multiple examples of each term using the class list from Step 2.

5. Distribute copies of *Taking the Oath of Office Primary Source Connection* activity sheet (pages 102–103) to students. Discuss the image as a class. Give students time to answer the questions concerning the picture with partners. Then, discuss the answers as a whole class.

6. Explain that tomorrow is Election Day! Students will have one last chance to think about the candidates before they go to the polls to cast their vote.

 ## 2 Day Conduct and Assess

Teacher Tip: Plan ahead. Cover a box (a shoe box will do) with plain wrapping paper or brown grocery bags to act as the ballot box. Label it with your name and a voting precinct number (e.g., Smith Precinct #007). If desired, ask student volunteers to further decorate the box. Place it on a table with room for students to line up, receive their ballot, and vote.

Lesson 8: Going to the Polls *(cont.)*

1. Set up your classroom to look like a voting precinct. Distribute copies of the *Voter Application* (page 105) to each student. As students enter the room, have them complete their application and turn it in. Once their application is received, they may have the *Voter Identification Card* (page 106). They should write their name on it and sign it. Explain that students will need to present their voter ID to receive their ballot.

Teacher Tip: Write your school name and precinct name and number on the voter identification cards prior to copying them.

2. Review the two party candidates: Mrs. E of the Triangle Party, and Mr. J of the Square Party. As a class, review what students already know about both candidates. They declared one party on their voter application. Explain that this does not mean they must vote for that party's candidate. Distribute copies of the *Candidate Values and Traits* activity sheet (page 104) to students. Have students work with a partner or in small groups to review each candidate's biographies. Then, they should list each candidate's values and traits on another sheet of paper. Students should discuss who they think makes a better candidate and justify their opinion.

3. Now it is time for students to go to the polls! They will choose their candidate for president: Mrs. E from the Triangle Party, or Mr. J from the Square Party. Have students line up at the voting precinct. They should present their voter ID, sign their name to receive their ballot, and vote in private at a carrel or in a private space in the room. Have them fold their ballot before placing it in the ballot box.

Teacher Tip: Have a printed class list available at the precinct. It should have lines after each student's name so he or she can sign that a ballot was received.

4. If possible, create "I Voted" stickers ahead of time using address labels. Or, call ahead to your local Supervisor of Elections office and ask if they have stickers you can hand out to your students. Allow students to wear the stickers after they vote.

5. Once the voting is complete, discuss how this experience compares to what adults experience when they vote in real elections. Explain to students that they will find out the results of the election during the next lesson.

6. Distribute copies of the *Going to the Polls Comprehension Check* activity sheet (page 108) to assess students' understanding of the voting process. Use the Comprehension Check Evaluation Rubric (page 15) to evaluate students' work.

 # Lesson 8: Going to the Polls (cont.)

Extension Ideas

✔ Find Out More

If a president is suspected of wrongdoing, he may be *impeached*. This means he is formally accused of wrongdoing. Once impeached, a president can be removed from office. But this has not happened in United States history to date. Have students learn about one president's impeachment proceedings (Johnson, Tyler, or Clinton) or resignation (Nixon). They can put a slide show together to summarize the actions that led to the impeachment or resignation, and the result of the impeachment.

✔ Research Extension

The way that citizens vote has changed greatly throughout the years. Ask students to research the various ways in which both voting polls and technology in voting have changed. Then, have students create artistic time lines to show these changes by including either drawings or pictures cut from magazines.

✔ Connecting Elections

Have students think about this quote: "If you don't vote, you give up the right to complain later" (author unknown). Tell students to explain what this quote means and whether or not they agree with it.

Name: _____ Date: _____

Going to the Polls Content-Area Vocabulary

Directions: Read the definitions. Explain the importance of each term. Then draw a picture to illustrate each word.

> **constitutional democracy**—a system of government that limits the power of government, set forth in a constitution
>
> **Election Day**—the day assigned for an election; polling day
>
> **trait**—a characteristic or quality of a person
>
> **value**—a principal or standard expected of people

Term	This is important because…	What it looks like (picture)
constitutional democracy		
Election Day		
trait		
value		

Name: _____ Date: _____

Going to the Polls Background Information

Election Day is an important day in the United States. American citizens will choose their next leaders! A new president is elected every four years. New representatives are elected every two years. New senators are elected every six years. But, they are not all elected at the same time. Some years, maybe just three or four are elected. Some are elected two years later. The rest are elected two years after that. This way, every state does not vote for all its senators and all its representatives in one day.

Election Day is always the Tuesday following the first Monday in November. This is because many people used to farm. They had to travel very far to get to the polls. November is a good month for farmers to travel. Their crops are usually done by then. Also, some people had to travel for more than one day to get to the polls. They could travel on Monday and Tuesday. They would still have time to vote.

The candidates have all campaigned hard to win over American voters. They want people to vote for them! But, how can voters know that they are voting for the right person? They should vote for the candidates who have the same **values** they do. This means that they believe the same things. They think the same way. For example, a voter

might believe that every American should have health care. Then, he or she should vote for the candidate who also believes this.

Besides common values, voters look for candidates to have certain personal **traits**. These are the qualities of a person. A strong candidate has a commitment to the ideas behind our **constitutional democracy**. A strong candidate respects the rights of others. A strong candidate can work with all different people. He or she is dependable and reliable. He or she is courageous and honest. He or she is fair, smart, and hard working. A strong candidate also has special knowledge or skills. He or she has experience working in government. The job will not be all new once he or she is elected.

How does a voter know if a candidate has these traits? Voters watch how candidates behave. They watch their commercials. They listen to what they say. They read interviews. They make judgments based on what they see and what they hear. If they do not like the candidate's personal traits, they might not vote for him or her. Sometimes, if voters do not like any candidates, they will not cast votes. This means there will be less voter turnout.

Name: _____ Date: _____

Going to the Polls

Directions: Use the information from the *Going to the Polls Background Information* activity sheet to complete this page.

Election Day is always the Tuesday following the first Monday in November. Look at these calendars. Put an X on the election days.

NOVEMBER 2000

Sun	Mon	Tues	Wed	Thurs	Fri	Sat
		1	2	3	4	5
7	8	9	10	11	12	13
14	15	16	17	18	19	20
21	22	23	24	25	26	27
28	29	30				

NOVEMBER 2004

Sun	Mon	Tues	Wed	Thurs	Fri	Sat
				1	2	3
4	5	6	7	8	9	10
11	12	13	14	15	16	17
18	19	20	21	22	23	24
25	26	27	28	29	30	

NOVEMBER 2008

Sun	Mon	Tues	Wed	Thurs	Fri	Sat
					1	2
3	4	5	6	7	8	9
10	11	12	13	14	15	16
17	18	19	20	21	22	23
24	25	26	27	28	29	30

NOVEMBER 2012

Sun	Mon	Tues	Wed	Thurs	Fri	Sat
30						1
2	3	4	5	6	7	8
9	10	11	12	13	14	15
16	17	18	19	20	21	22
23	24	25	26	27	28	29

If you were voting for the next president, what **values** would you want this person to have? What **traits** would you want this person to have? Write your ideas here.

Values for a Presidential Candidate	Personal Traits of a Presidential Candidate

Name: _____ Date: _____

Taking the Oath of Office Primary Source Connection

Directions: Read the information below.

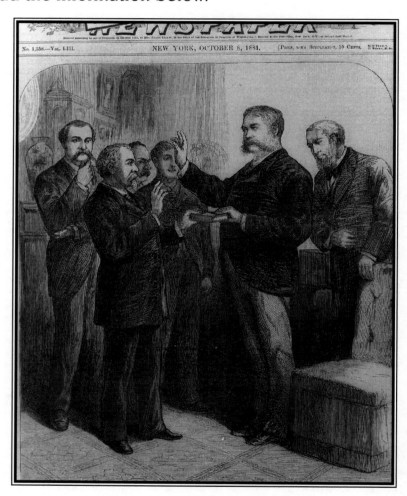

Primary Source Background Information

This picture shows Judge Brady administering the Presidential Oath of Office to Vice President Chester A. Arthur. Arthur was sworn into office in 1881 following the death of President James A. Garfield. Presidents take this oath with their hand on the Bible.

Presidential Oath of Office: "I do solemnly swear (or affirm) that I will faithfully execute the Office of President of the United States, and will to the best of my ability, preserve, protect, and defend the Constitution of the United States."

Taking the Oath of Office Primary Source Connection (cont.)

Primary Source Questions

Directions: Look at the picture. Answer the questions below.

1. Describe the scene in the picture.

_____

_____

2. What do the other men in the picture seem to be thinking?

_____

_____

3. Voters often go to the polls to vote for a president, not thinking that perhaps the vice presidential candidate will become president within the four years. How do you think the values and traits of the vice president compare to the president?

_____

_____

_____

4. How does the Presidential Oath of Office reflect a candidate's need to have strong values and personal traits?

_____

_____

_____

Primary Source Extension

James A. Garfield was not the first president to die while in office, nor was he the last. Find out which other presidents died in office, and who took over for them.

Name: _____ Date: _____

Candidate Values and Traits

Directions: Think about the two candidates running for president. Read their biographies below. On a separate sheet of paper, list the values they hold and the personal traits they show. Decide which candidate you believe holds your values and shows personal traits you admire. Get ready to vote. You will help elect the next president!

Mrs. E's Biography (Triangle Party Candidate)

Triangle Party member for 12 years.

Was an ordinary citizen before getting into politics.

Believes in personal responsibility.

Began a privately run, community organization to keep forests clean.

Elected governor of her state.

Is careful spending tax dollars.

Believes government should be run by the people.

Is very smart and a quick thinker.

Is sly and confident. Can seem deceitful at times, but has never been in trouble with the law.

Mr. J's Biography (Square Party Candidate)

Square Party member for ten years.

Comes from a long line of Square Party members. Family was in politics, too.

Believes in strong government rules and regulations.

Headed first State Litter Control Board.

Helped pass first tough anti litter laws.

Continues working at the state level with senators, representatives, and the governor.

Is flexible and quiet. Can seem shy at times, but gets along well with almost everyone.

Takes advantage of opportunities when he sees them, so can seem selfish at times.

Is hard working.

Voter Application

Teacher Directions: Cut out the applications below and distribute them to the students.

Voter Application

Directions: Fill out this application to register to vote. Turn it into the elections office (your teacher). Get your Voter Identification Card. Keep it with you. You will need your Voter ID to vote.

Name _____ **Date** _____

Address _____

_____

Telephone Number _____

Date of Birth _____ **Gender (circle one)**   M   F

Are you a United States citizen? _____ Yes _____ No

Are you 18 years old or older? _____ Yes _____ No

Have you been convicted of a felony? _____ Yes _____ No

To which party do you belong? _____ Triangle _____ Square _____ Other/Name

Voter Application

Directions: Fill out this application to register to vote. Turn it into the elections office (your teacher). Get your Voter Identification Card. Keep it with you. You will need your Voter ID to vote.

Name _____ **Date** _____

Address _____

_____

Telephone Number _____

Date of Birth _____ **Gender (circle one)**   M   F

Are you a United States citizen? _____ Yes _____ No

Are you 18 years old or older? _____ Yes _____ No

Have you been convicted of a felony? _____ Yes _____ No

To which party do you belong? _____ Triangle _____ Square _____ Other/Name

Voter Identification Cards

Teacher Directions: Cut out the cards below and distribute them to the students.

Voter Identification Card

Name _____

School _____

Signature _____

Assigned Precinct _____

Voter Identification Card

Name _____

School _____

Signature _____

Assigned Precinct _____

Voter Identification Card

Name _____

School _____

Signature _____

Assigned Precinct _____

Voter Identification Card

Name _____

School _____

Signature _____

Assigned Precinct _____

Voter Identification Card

Name _____

School _____

Signature _____

Assigned Precinct _____

Voter Identification Card

Name _____

School _____

Signature _____

Assigned Precinct _____

Voting Ballots

Teacher Directions: Cut out the ballots below. Distribute them to your students.

Voting Ballot

Place an X in front of the ONE candidate for whom you are voting. Fold the ballot and place it in the ballot box.

_____ Mrs. E   Triangle Party

_____ Mr. J   Square Party

_____ Write-in Candidate: _____

Voting Ballot

Place an X in front of the ONE candidate for whom you are voting. Fold the ballot and place it in the ballot box.

_____ Mrs. E   Triangle Party

_____ Mr. J   Square Party

_____ Write-in Candidate: _____

Voting Ballot

Place an X in front of the ONE candidate for whom you are voting. Fold the ballot and place it in the ballot box.

_____ Mrs. E   Triangle Party

_____ Mr. J   Square Party

_____ Write-in Candidate: _____

Voting Ballot

Place an X in front of the ONE candidate for whom you are voting. Fold the ballot and place it in the ballot box.

_____ Mrs. E   Triangle Party

_____ Mr. J   Square Party

_____ Write-in Candidate: _____

Name: _____ Date: _____

Going to the Polls Comprehension Check

Directions: On a separate sheet of paper, answer the questions below according to the directions from your teacher.

★ Remember

When is Election Day?

★ Understand

Why is it important for a presidential candidate to value a constitutional democracy?

★ Apply

You have an opportunity to help at the polls during the next general election. Would you accept this offer? Explain why or why not.

★ Analyze

Think about your voting experience. Write a journal entry explaining how you felt when you voted, why you believe your vote made a difference or not, and whether believe the voting process in which you participated was fair.

★ Evaluate

What five personal traits do you believe are the most important when considering a candidate for public office? Explain why you listed each trait.

★ Create

Create a song about voting. Include five or more words that have to do with elections. Put your song to a familiar tune, such as "Yankee Doodle" or "Twinkle, Twinkle, Little Star."

 # Lesson 9: Elected Leaders in Action

Standards

- Students know what political leaders do and why leadership is necessary in a democracy (McREL Civics 29.1)
- Students know the major duties, powers, privileges, and limitations of a position of leadership, and knows how to evaluate the strengths and weaknesses of candidates in terms of the qualifications required for a particular leadership role (McREL Civics 29.4)

Vocabulary

- Congress
- elector
- executive branch
- Inauguration Day
- treaty
- veto

Materials

- *Elected Leaders in Action Content-Area Vocabulary* (page 113)
- *Elected Leaders in Action Background Information* (page 114)
- *Elected Leaders in Action Graphic Organizer* (page 115)
- *Lincoln with His Cabinet Primary Source Connection* (pages 116–117)
- *Leadership from the Triangle Party President* (pages 118–119) or *Leadership from the Square Party President* (pages 120–121)
- *Elected Leaders in Action Comprehension Check* (page 122)

 ## Introduce the Content

Day 1

1. Begin class by having students reflect on their voting experience. Have them turn to a partner and discuss whether they liked or disliked the voting experience and why.

2. Tell students that the votes have been counted, and they have a new president. But, this person will not take over the office for some time, yet. Discuss as a class why this may be so.

3. Distribute copies of the *Elected Leaders in Action Content-Area Vocabulary* activity sheet (page 113) to students. Read the definitions as a class. Read the directions. Complete the first two terms as a class. Then, allow students to work with a partner to complete the remaining terms. You may also ask students to complete one of the following Vocabulary Extension Activities.

✔ Vocabulary Extension Activities

- Have students illustrate their vocabulary comparisons. They should include at least two characters, with dialogue, to help explain the comparison.

- Have students write three or more examples for each of the words. For example, students might list *representative*, *hired*, or *voter* for *elector*.

 # Lesson 9: Elected Leaders in Action *(cont.)*

4. Distribute copies of the *Elected Leaders in Action Background Information* (page 114) and the *Elected Leaders in Action Graphic Organizer* (page 115) activity sheets to students. Allow them to read the information in small groups. After reading, ask the groups to list the steps the government follows to formally assign a newly elected president to office. Discuss the steps as a whole class.

5. Discuss the differences between the *executive branch* and the *legislative branch* of government, and how one cannot exist without the other. If desired, this lesson can lead into a more detailed study of the three branches of government and the balance of powers.

6. Have students consider the qualities a president might look for in a Cabinet leader. Distribute copies of the *Lincoln with His Cabinet Primary Source Connection* activity sheet (pages 116–117) to students. Review the picture and caption as a class. Have students answer the questions with a small group.

Differentiation Idea

Have **English language learners** work with a proficient English-speaking partner. Have them collaborate to highlight the people or groups that are part of the executive and legislative branches of government. Be sure that both **below-level** students and English language learners understand the difference between the executive and legislative branches of government. Illustrate these ideas, if needed.

 # Conduct and Assess

Teacher Note: If desired, after sharing the election results (see Step 2), explain that red is the Republican party color, and blue is the Democratic party color. When students see these colors on a presidential election map, they know which candidate has won that state. Also explain that states are considered "red" or "blue" states, depending on the number of registered voters from each party in each state.

1. Have students discuss with a partner to review what they learned about how a president must work with his or her Congress to enforce the laws.

2. Post the election results from Lesson 8. After all the excitement ebbs, explain that the work of the president is just beginning. Assign one person to act as President E (if the Triangle Party candidate won) or President J (if the Square Party candidate won). Then, divide the class into two groups: the House of Representatives and the Senate. Be sure members from both parties are included in each group.

Lesson 9: Elected Leaders in Action *(cont.)*

3. Distribute copes of either the *Leadership from the Triangle Party President* (pages 118–119) or the *Leadership from the Square Party President* (pages 120–121) activity sheet to students, depending on which candidate won the election. Read the directions as a class. Then, walk through the simulation as a class. The president should act out his or her role. Then, while the House of Representatives members are discussing the bill (Step 2), the Senate should listen. While the Senate discusses the bill (Step 3), the House should listen. If and when the bill passes both houses, have the person acting as president sign it or veto it.

4. Discuss this process as a class. Explain that one crucial step that is not part of the simulation is committee work. The House and Senate do not necessarily do all the work on bills. Committee members work on the bills, then submit them to the appropriate house for approval or discussion.

5. Have students answer the questions with a partner or in small groups.

Differentiation Idea

Have **above-level** students research a law that the current president has recently signed. Students who complete this activity can share the bill that was originally introduced, and follow it through committees and both houses as it made its way to the president. Or, students can research bills that have been vetoed by the president. Students who complete this activity can share the bill and explain why the president vetoed it.

6. Distribute copies of the *Elected Leaders in Action Comprehension Check* activity sheet (page 122) to assess students' understanding of the work presidents conduct in office. Use the Comprehension Check Evaluation Rubric (page 15) to evaluate students' work.

Extension Ideas

 Find Out More

Every leader has certain duties, powers, privileges, and limitations. Have students find out more about their state governor's powers and limitations, and compare them to those of the president.

Extension Ideas

Research Extension

The executive and legislative branches of government are joined by the judicial branch. Have students find out more about this third arm of the government. They should explain who it includes, what the major duties are of this branch, and how its members work with the president and Congress to help run the government.

 Lesson 9: Elected Leaders in Action *(cont.)*

Extension Ideas *(cont.)*

✔ Connecting Elections

Taking on a leadership role can be exciting, but scary. Have students write about a time when they took on a leadership role. Perhaps they were a team captain. Perhaps their mom put them in charge of a younger sibling. Perhaps they decided what was for dinner one night. Students should write their personal narrative detailing their major duties, powers, privileges, and limitations while serving in this leadership role.

Name: _____ Date: _____

Elected Leaders in Action Content-Area Vocabulary

Directions: Read the definitions for each word. Think about how each word compares to something else. Use the ideas in the Idea Box.

Example: An <u>elector</u> is like a <u>baseball player</u> because they go up to vote for presidents following their lineup just like baseball players.

Congress—the national legislative body of the United States that includes the Senate and the House of Representatives

elector—a citizen chosen to vote for the president and vice president of the United States, representing a group of people

executive branch—the branch of the United States government that carries out laws

Inauguration Day—the day the next United States president is sworn into office

---

Idea Box

gumball	firecracker	basketball team	fishing	bus ride
envelope	camera	video game	phone call	pizza

---

1. Congress is like a _____ because _____

_____ .

2. An elector is like a _____ because _____

_____ .

3. The executive branch is like a _____ because _____

_____ .

4. Inauguration Day is like a _____ because _____

_____ .

Name: _____ Date: _____

Elected Leaders in Action Background Information

A presidential candidate may have thought running a campaign was a lot of work. Now that he or she has been elected president, the work really begins! A lot happens between Election Day and **Inauguration Day**. First, states must certify their votes. This means that they state that they are certain the votes are correct. They have a deadline to do this. The deadline is in December. Then, the **electors** from each state meet. The electors cast their votes for president. Electors are people who represent the states. They cast votes based on the population of their state. Electors cast these votes in December. In early January, the current vice president runs a meeting in **Congress**. He or she calls each state by name. They are called in alphabetical order. The votes are read aloud. They are counted. The winner is announced.

The voting is finally over. But the job does not start yet. The new president is called the president-elect. He or she must take the Oath of Office. This takes place on January 20 at noon. It is administered by the Chief Justice. This person is on the United States Supreme Court. This swearing-in ceremony is called an inauguration. Now, the new president can take over!

What does a president do? The president makes up the **executive branch** of government. This person makes sure that laws are obeyed. The president has help from his or her vice president. Cabinet members also help the president. One person is the Secretary of the Treasury. This person oversees America's taxes and money. Another cabinet member is the Secretary of the Interior. This person makes sure natural resources and wildlife are protected.

The president signs bills into laws. Bills come from Congress. They make the laws. Bills are statements that people want to become law. If the president does not like the bill, he or she **vetoes** it. This means it does not become law.

The president meets with leaders around the world. Together, they talk about how the two governments can work together. They may even write **treaties**. The treaties are not official until Congress approves them. The president is also the Commander in Chief. He or she is the boss of the military. The president can decide when to use American troops. He or she does not need to declare war to do this. Congress must approve an official declaration of war. The president needs Congress and America needs the president.

Name: _____ Date: _____

Elected Leaders in Action Graphic Organizer

Directions: Use the information from the *Elected Leaders in Action Background Information* activity sheet. List the responsibilities of the president, vice president, cabinet, and Congress in the chart below. Then, answer the questions below.

Executive Branch			Legislative Branch
President	**Vice President**	**Cabinet**	**Congress**

1. Why does the president need Congress?

_____

_____

2. Why does Congress need the president?

_____

_____

3. Why is leadership necessary in a constitutional democracy?

_____

_____

Name: _____ Date: _____

Lincoln with His Cabinet Primary Source Connection

Directions: Read the information below.

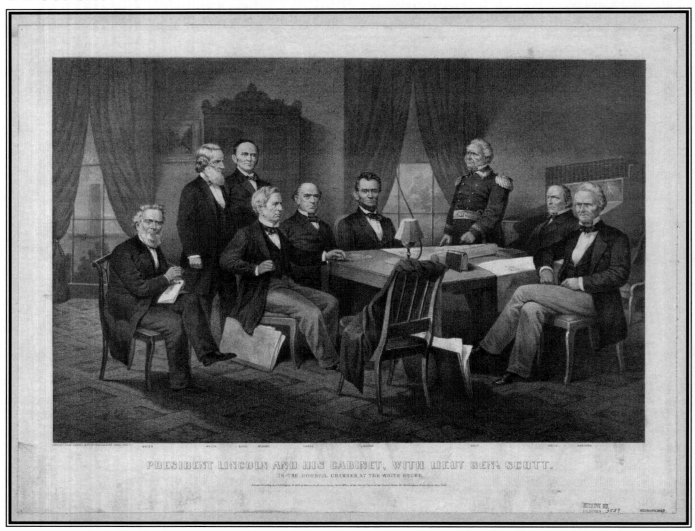

PRESIDENT LINCOLN AND HIS CABINET, WITH LIEUT GENL SCOTT.
IN THE COUNCIL CHAMBER AT THE WHITE HOUSE.

Primary Source Background Information

This picture shows President Abraham Lincoln seated with his Cabinet members. Lincoln was president from 1861 to 1865. Also in the picture is Lieutenant General Winfield Scott. He was in the War of 1812. He was in the Civil War. He served in many wars in between these two wars, as well. Scott ran for president in 1852. But, he lost the election. He was the commanding general of the United States Army for 20 years.

Lincoln with His Cabinet Primary Source Connection *(cont.)*

Primary Source Questions

Directions: Look at the picture. Answer the questions below.

1. Abraham Lincoln is seated at the desk. There are papers scattered on and around the desk. What do you think these might be about?

_____

_____

_____

2. Why do you think Lincoln chose these men to be his cabinet leaders?

_____

_____

_____

3. How do you think this scene would compare to today's president meeting with his or her cabinet members?

_____

_____

_____

Primary Source Extension

If you were president, whom would you want to lead your Cabinet? On a separate sheet of paper, list three people who you would want to serve by your side. Explain why these people would make good cabinet leaders.

Name: _____ Date: _____

Leadership from the Triangle Party President

Directions: The Triangle Party presidential candidate has won the election! Now, Mrs. E must work with Congress to keep the government running smoothly. Unfortunately, some members of Congress disagree with a new bill. Follow these steps to find out what happens. Then, answer the questions on the next page.

Step 1

President E asks a Triangle Party member of the House of Representatives to introduce this bill: *Forestland needs a new hospital for sick and injured animals. Mrs. E wants to pass a law that would lower the tax rate for hospital companies. These companies would then use the money they would have paid in taxes to build the new hospital.*

Step 2

A Triangle Party House of Representatives member introduces the bill. Talk as a group. You have three choices. You can:

1. Pass the bill as it reads. Discuss it. Vote on it. More than half the House members must agree. Once agreed, pass it along to the Senate. Go to Step 3.

2. Change the bill and vote again on it. More than half the House members must agree to the changes. Once agreed, pass it along to the Senate. Go to Step 3.

3. Not accept the bill. It "dies" with the House of Representatives. The Senate does not get to vote at all. You are done. Answer the questions on the next page.

Step 3

Once a bill passes the House of Representatives, it goes to the Senate. Talk as a group. You have three choices. You can:

1. Pass the bill as it reads. Discuss it. Vote on it. More than half the Senate members must agree. Once agreed, pass it along to President E. Go to Step 4.

2. Change the bill and vote again on it. More than half the Senate members must agree to the changes. Once agreed, pass it back to the House of Representatives. Go back to Step 2.

3. Not accept the bill. It "dies" with the Senate. You are done. Answer the questions.

Leadership from the Triangle Party President *(cont.)*

Step 4

Once the Senate passes the bill, it goes to President E for her signature. She has two choices. She can:

- Sign the bill. Now, the bill becomes law.

- Reject the changes. Veto the bill. It "dies" with President E.

Questions:

1. Who was the leader in Step 1?

_____

2. Who was the leader in Steps 2 and 3?

_____

3. Who was the leader in Step 4?

_____

4. Do you think Mrs. E has power? Explain your answer.

_____

_____

_____

5. Do you think Congress has power? Explain your answer.

_____

_____

_____

6. What are your thoughts about the steps a bill takes to become a law?

_____

_____

Name: _____ Date: _____

Leadership from the Square Party President

Directions: The Square Party presidential candidate has won the election! Now, Mr. J must work with Congress to keep the government running smoothly. Unfortunately, some members of Congress disagree with a new bill. Follow these steps to find out what happens. Then, answer the questions on the next page.

Step 1

President J asks a Square Party member of the House of Representatives to introduce this bill: *Wetland City needs a new hospital for sick and injured animals. Mr. J wants to pass a law that would raise the tax rate for hospital companies. The government would then use this tax money to build and run this new hospital.*

Step 2

A Square Party House of Representatives member introduces the bill. Talk as a group. You have three choices. You can:

1. Pass the bill as it reads. Discuss it. Vote on it. More than half the House members must agree. Once agreed, pass it along to the Senate. Go to Step 3.

2. Change the bill and vote again on it. More than half the House members must agree to the changes. Once agreed, pass it along to the Senate. Go to Step 3.

3. Not accept the bill. It "dies" with the House of Representatives. The Senate does not get to vote at all. You are done. Answer the questions on the next page.

Step 3

Once a bill passes the House of Representatives, it goes to the Senate. Talk as a group. You have three choices. You can:

1. Pass the bill as it reads. Discuss it. Vote on it. More than half the Senate members must agree. Once agreed, pass it along to President J. Go to Step 4.

2. Change the bill and vote again on it. More than half the Senate members must agree to the changes. Once agreed, pass it back to the House of Representatives. Go back to Step 2.

3. Not accept the bill. It "dies" with the Senate. You are done. Answer the questions.

Leadership from the Square Party President *(cont.)*

Step 4

Once the Senate passes the bill, it goes to President J for his signature. He has two choices. He can:

- Sign the bill. Now, the bill becomes law.
- Reject the changes. Veto the bill. It "dies" with President E.

Questions:

1. Who was the leader in Step 1?

_____

2. Who was the leader in Steps 2 and 3?

_____

3. Who was the leader in Step 4?

_____

4. Do you think Mr. J has power? Explain your answer.

_____

_____

_____

5. Do you think Congress has power? Explain your answer.

_____

_____

_____

6. What are your thoughts about the steps a bill takes to become a law?

_____

_____

Name: _____ Date: _____

Elected Leaders in Action Comprehension Check

Directions: On a separate sheet of paper, answer the questions according to the directions from your teacher.

★ Remember

Write three major duties of the president.

★ Understand

Explain how a president relies on his or her cabinet and Congress to run the government.

★ Apply

Write a diary entry as if you were the president wanting to pass a bill that you favor into law. Describe your feelings as the bill enters the House of Representatives and follows the steps to be placed on your desk for your signature.

★ Analyze

Some people refer to the president as "the most powerful person on Earth." Do you agree or disagree with this statement? Explain your answer.

★ Evaluate

Think about how a president must rely on Congress, and how Congress must rely on the president. Explain why this system creates a strong, balanced government that supports a constitutional democracy.

★ Create

Make a cartoon to show the steps a bill follows to become a law. Include dialogue in speech bubbles.

 # Lesson 10: Doing My Part

Standard

- Students know opportunities for leadership and public service in the student's own classroom, school, community, state, and the nation; and understand why leadership and public service are important to the continuance and improvement of American democracy (McREL Civics 29.2)

- Students understand the importance of individuals working cooperatively with their elected leaders (McREL Civics 29.3)

Vocabulary

- collaborate
- community
- nonprofit
- organization
- public
- volunteer

Materials

- *Doing My Part Content-Area Vocabulary* (page 126)

- *Doing My Part Background Information* (page 127)

- *Doing My Part Graphic Organizer* (page 128)

- *Volunteering on the Home Front Primary Source Connection* (pages 129–130)

- *Collaborate to Succeed* (page 131)

- *Doing My Part Comprehension Check* (page 132)

- Paper or online newspaper articles (*optional*)

 ## Introduce the Content

1. In Lesson 5, students learned how citizens could get involved in campaigns. Even though they are not the ones running for election, their involvement can help influence government decisions. Review how citizens' involvement in elections leads to continued improvement of the government.

2. Explain that after the election, citizens can stay involved. They can continue to be part of politics through political organizations, or they can get involved in their community. There are many leadership opportunities for many people. Have students turn to a partner and list ways they think citizens might stay involved after an election.

3. Distribute copies of the *Doing My Part Content-Area Vocabulary* activity sheet (page 126) to students. Read the definitions as a class. Have students complete this activity sheet independently or with a partner.

Lesson 10: Doing My Part *(cont.)*

Differentiation Idea

Work with **English language learners** in a small group to complete the vocabulary activity sheet. If possible, provide pictures to show examples of each term, or discuss the terms and what each might look like. Support their efforts to write one complete sentence for each term.

✔ Vocabulary Extension Activities

- Ask students to use at least three of the vocabulary terms to create an advertisement for a real or imagined community organization.

- Have students think about how volunteers help their community. Have students write a diary entry from the perspective of someone who benefited from volunteer efforts. Students should use at least three of the vocabulary terms in their diary entries.

4. Distribute copies of the *Doing My Part Background Information* (page 127) and the *Doing My Part Graphic Organizer* (page 128) activity sheets to students. Read the information to the class as they follow along. List three ways people can stay involved in government after an election (e.g., volunteering, getting a job with a government group, joining an organization). Discuss similarities and differences among these three ideas. Have students complete the student activity sheet independently or with a partner.

5. Distribute copies of the *Volunteering on the Home Front Primary Source Connection* activity sheet (pages 129–130) to students. Have students read the information in small groups. Discuss as a class how the volunteers made a difference in their community. Have students answer the questions on the activity sheets with their group.

Conduct and Assess

1. Review from Day 1 different ways people can stay involved in government after an election. Write the word *collaboration* on the board. Have students talk with a partner to discuss why this idea is essential for any involvement activity.

2. Have students turn to a partner. They should share a time when they disagreed with a decision and how they attempted to make their position known. They should also explain how they worked collaboratively, and whether they were successful or not in changing the other person's mind.

Lesson 10: Doing My Part *(cont.)*

3. Explain that many times citizens get involved because they are concerned about a situation or a decision. They want to know that they have a voice. They want to persuade others to understand their side. Distribute copies of the *Collaborate to Succeed* activity sheet (page 131) to students. Read the directions as a class. Have students work in groups of four. Once all the groups have finished, discuss the issues as a class. Have students identify how citizens in each situation must collaborate to achieve their goal.

Differentiation Idea

Clarify each situation for **English language learners**. Be sure they understand what a school board and sheriff are, and which citizens are affected by each situation.

4. Distribute copies of the *Doing My Part Comprehension Check* activity sheet (page 132) to assess students' understanding of how citizens can stay involved after an election. Use the Comprehension Check Evaluation Rubric (page 15) to evaluate students' work.

Extension Ideas

✔ Find Out More

Have students find out about community organizations where they live. They should bring in a list of the organizations, their missions, and recent events. Students can publish this information on a flyer using an electronic publishing program.

✔ Research Extension

Have students call or email a locally elected official to find out what topics are on an upcoming agenda, either at a school board meeting, or at a city council meeting. They might also discover this information online if the agendas are published ahead of time. Students can report to the class what the situation is, which citizens are directly affected, and possible solutions. They might also report how the elected officials collaborate to reach their goals.

✔ Connecting Elections

Have students think about a person they know who volunteers, has a government job, or is involved in a community organization. Have them write a personal journal entry explaining who this person is, and how his or her involvement helps improve and continue our American democracy.

Name: _____ Date: _____

Doing My Part Content-Area Vocabulary

Directions: Use the definitions below to illustrate each vocabulary term. Write a sentence with the term to explain your picture.

---

collaborate—to work together; cooperate; act as a team

community—a group of people living in the same area and under the same government

nonprofit—not for making money; charitable

organization—a group of people that comes together for a purpose

public—a community of people; not private

volunteer—to do something of a person's own free will; unpaid worker

---

Vocabulary Term	Illustration	Sentence
collaborate		
community		
nonprofit		
organization		
public		
volunteer		

Name: _____ Date: _____

Doing My Part Background Information

Elected officials have an important job to do. They must work to run the government. This is a big responsibility. They must work with many people, even when they do not agree. But, they cannot do everything by themselves. Citizens can do their part to stay involved after the election is over. They can help make sure our American democracy carries on. They can help make sure it improves. This helps everyone.

Two ways citizens can get involved is to join local school board meetings. Or, they can join city council meetings. These are open to the **public**. A school board discusses items that have to do with how schools are run. They may discuss new building projects. They may discuss new bus routes. Their decisions affect students, parents, and teachers. City council members talk about new building projects. They talk about protected land. They talk about how to improve their community. Their decisions affect you and your family.

There are many more ways in which citizens can take part in the work of the government. People can work in jobs that are run by the government. They are policemen and firemen. They are teachers and city workers. These people are not elected, but they are part of a group that is run by the government. They can make little changes that make a big difference. People can also **volunteer**. There is always plenty of work that needs to be done! Volunteers give time to their community. They do not get paid for their time. They are an important part of the community by joining **nonprofits**. People can also join clubs and organizations. Many clubs support the community. They **collaborate** to help others know the history of your area.

You might not think of yourself as a leader, but you are! Maybe you have led a soccer or baseball team. Maybe you made a suggestion at school and something was changed. Maybe you planned games at your house during a sleepover. These are all examples of leadership. Some people your age are part of scouts or 4H. These **organizations** give children many chances to lead their peers. Some children get involved in **community** events. They volunteer at the library or the local zoo. Or, they might help with a neighborhood cleanup project. They help make it a better place to live. Some children raise funds for local charities. They might ask for donations to give to their local food pantry or family support center. All these children volunteers have their parents' permission to help.

Name: _____ Date: _____

Doing My Part Graphic Organizer

Directions: There are many ways people can stay involved in government, even after an election. Use the details from the *Doing My Part Background Information* sheet (page 127). List details in the middle box about each way that people can stay involved. Draw a picture for each way in the bottom box.

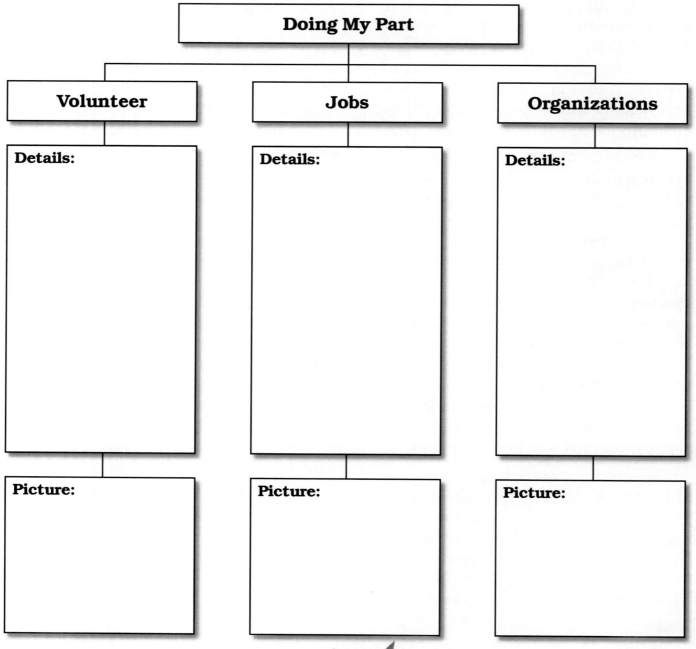

Name: _____ Date: _____

Volunteering on the Home Front Primary Source Connection

Directions: Read the information below.

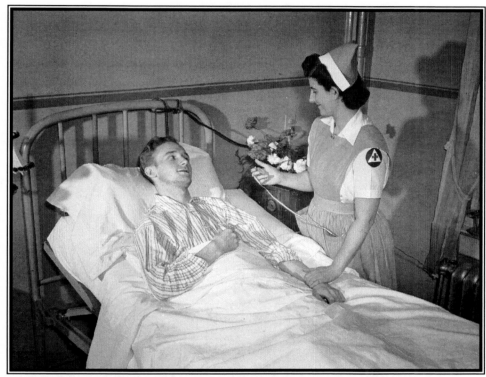

Primary Source Background Information

This photo is from 1942. This was a time when America was at war. There was a shortage of nurse's aides. The government called for 100,000 people to step forward and volunteer! This aide is working at Freedmen's Hospital in Washington, DC. Volunteers here went through an 80-hour training course. These volunteers worked directly with nurses and doctors. Other duties included changing beds, feeding patients, dressing wounds, giving baths, taking temperatures and pulses, and packing surgical kits.

Name: _____ Date: _____

Volunteering on the Home Front Primary Source Connection *(cont.)*
Primary Source Questions

Directions: Look at the picture. Answer the questions below.

1. Why is the woman in the picture volunteering?

_____

_____

_____

2. Why was her volunteer work so important?

_____

_____

_____

3. What might have happened had others, not volunteered their time as nurse's aides?

_____

_____

_____

Primary Source Extension

What would you say to this women, if you could have met her? On a separate sheet of paper, write a letter to share your appreciation for her work.

Name: _____ Date: _____

Collaborate to Succeed

Directions: There are many ways people can stay involved in government. No matter how it is done, people must work together. Think about these situations. On a separate sheet of paper, decide how each group might go about collaborating to achieve its goal. Use the guiding questions to lead you.

Situation 1

A school board needs to reduce expenses. One way to do this is to reduce printing costs. They are thinking about "hiring" inmates at a nearby prison to do most or all of the school district's printing. This will save an estimated $500,000 of tax payer dollars each year by hiring inmates. Owners of printing businesses are upset because they will lose business. The school district is one of their largest accounts. School leaders are also upset because the prison takes too long to print things. Oftentimes they cannot wait weeks for their printing needs.

Situation 2

Sheriff Dorn is concerned. When his officers stop a teenager for doing something wrong, they cannot see records to show if he or she has been ticketed before. This means that repeat offenders may get away without a ticket. Instead, they should be brought home or sent to lockup, depending on the crimes. Dorn is asking for quick and easy access to juvenile records for his officers. He wants to keep the community safe. A bill passed the state House of Representatives and Senate. But, Governor Todd vetoed the bill. She said it did not do enough to keep juvenile records confidential.

Guiding Questions

1. Who are the leaders?

2. What is the problem?

3. Which citizens are directly affected by this problem?

4. What is one outcome?

5. Who compromised to reach this solution?

6. What is another outcome?

7. Who compromised to reach this solution?

Name: _____ Date: _____

Doing My Part Comprehension Check

Directions: On a separate sheet of paper, answer the questions below according to the directions from your teacher.

★ Remember

List three ways young people can take on leadership roles.

★ Understand

Explain why collaboration is a key part of any attempt to do government work.

★ Apply

Create a brochure for a real or imaginary community organization. Explain the name of the organization, what they work to do, when and where they meet, and how others can get involved.

★ Analyze

Show how the work of elected officials compares to the work of citizens involved in government or citizens who take on leadership roles. Use a Venn diagram. List the work they do and how they do it. Explain what their goals are and how they go about reaching them.

★ Evaluate

On a scale of 1 to 5 (5 = very important, 1 = not important), how important do you think volunteers are to help our government run? Justify your rating.

★ Create

Write a newspaper article detailing a fictitious situation involving government. Explain what the situation is, who is involved, and how leaders propose to resolve the issue. Also, explain how this situation affects citizens, and what they are doing to reach their goals.

Answer Key

Political Parties Content-Area Vocabulary (page 20)

1. Democratic Party; Republican Party
2. government
3. political party
4. liberal
5. conservative

Political Parties Graphic Organizer (page 22)

Democrats: liberal; give freely; strong government; opportunities for everyone; economic growth; affordable health care; social groups; donkey

Republicans: began in 1854 over slavery; conservative; careful about giving things freely; people make America strong; personal responsibility; careful with money; money should stay with the people who earn it; limited services; national pride; elephant

Both: main political parties; have candidates; work in government; politicians

1. Democrats are more like the Federalists. They wanted a strong central government and power.

Political Parties Primary Source Connection (page 24)

1. Answers will vary.
2. Rear Admiral Winfield S. Schley; he is the winning leader of the Democratic Party
3. Answers will vary.

My Party Candidate (pages 25–26)

Students' posters will vary, but should represent their party's candidate appropriately. Check for understanding.

Political Parties Comprehension Check (page 27)

Students' answers will vary.

The Presidential Election Content-Area Vocabulary (page 32)

1. eligible
2. Constitution
3. term
4. qualify

Students' drawings will vary.

The Presidential Election Graphic Organizer (page 34)

President: born in the United States; at least 35 years old; lived in the U.S. for the past 14 years

Vice President: lived in the U.S. for the past 7 years; at least 30 years old; cannot live in the same state as the presidential candidate

1. voting; holding public office
2. Answers will vary.
3. Answers will vary.

The Constitution Rules Primary Source Connection (pages 35–36)

1. Answers will vary.
2. Answers will vary.
3. Answers will vary.

Who Is Eligible? (page 37)

James West: no; not born in the United States

Cindy East: yes; she is 30 or older; has lived in the U.S. for more than 7 years; however, do not know if she lives in the same state as her presidential running mate

Gerald North: no; has not lived in the U.S. for 7 years; unknown if he lives in the same state as running mate

Vera South: yes; she is over 35; born in U.S.; has lived in U.S. for over the past 14 years

The Presidential Election Comprehension Check (page 38)

Students' answers will vary.

State and Local Elections Content-Area Vocabulary (page 42)

1. senator
2. representative
3. mayor
4. governor
5. office
6. citizen
7. governor; office
8. citizens; mayor
9. senators; representatives

State and Local Leaders Graphic Organizer (page 44)

State Leaders: governor and lieutenant governor; must be eligible to run for office; elected by citizens of the state

Local Leaders: mayor; must qualify to run for office; elected by citizens of the town

Answer Key *(cont.)*

Mayor's Parade Primary Source Connection (page 46)

1. One of the mayor's responsibilities is to participate in special ceremonies.
2. There are a lot of people; everyone is well-dressed; people appear to be cheering and happy.
3. The mayor runs the city and represents the citizens of the city.

My State and Local Leaders (page 47)

Students' responses will vary based on their local and state leaders at the time.

State and Local Elections Comprehension Check (page 48)

Students' answers will vary.

The Candidates Content-Area Vocabulary (page 52)

Students' personal definitions and examples will vary.

The Candidates Graphic Organizer (page 54)

Candidates do the following things:

- run ads on television and the radio
- advertise on billboards and signs
- speak about their ideas

Voters can do the following things:

- help with elections
- hear the candidates speak
- join a group that needs political support

1. Voters should vote for the person they like the best, so they need to know why they like one candidate over another before they vote.
2. Answers will vary; however, students should understand that politics is all about making promises in exchange for special favors. They need support from each other to get what they want.

James K. Polk: Presidential Candidate Primary Source Connection (pages 55–56)

1. Polk is standing in a fancy room with his right arm extended.
2. Most candidates have real pictures, not hand-colored prints.
3. Yes, this was an effective slogan. Polk won the presidential election.

James K. Polk: Presidential Candidate Primary Source Connection *(cont.)* (pages 55–56)

4. Answers will vary; ideas include, but are not limited to, traveled on trains; spoke at meetings; had parades and special events.

Meet the Triangle Party Candidate (page 57)

Students' answers will vary.

Meet the Square Party Candidate (page 58)

Students' answers will vary.

The Candidate Comprehension Check (page 59)

Students' answers will vary.

On the Campaign Trail Content-Area Vocabulary (page 64)

1. campaign
2. represent
3. media
4. strategy
5. issue
6. debate

On the Campaign Trail Graphic Organizer (page 66)

Strategy: a plan of action; billboards; slogans, signs; advertise on the radio and television

Issues: a public concern; speeches; debates

Media: a way to report; reports on the news

Campaign Craze Primary Source Connection (page 68)

1. The picture shows political campaign signs.
2. Answers will vary.
3. Answers will vary.
4. Answers will vary.
5. Answers will vary.

My Triangle Party Candidate's Campaign (page 69)

Students' answers will vary.

My Square Party Candidate's Campaign (page 70)

Students' answers will vary.

Campaign Contribution List (page 71)

Students' answers will vary.

Answer Key *(cont.)*

On the Campaign Trail Comprehension Check (page 72)

Students' answers will vary.

Making a Difference Content-Area Vocabulary (page 77)

Examples and nonexamples for each term will vary.

1. interest group
2. demonstration
3. petition
4. forum
5. influence
6. rally

Making a Difference Graphic Organizer (page 79)

Any six: run for office; vote; join a campaign; volunteer for a candidate; join an interest group; join a political party club; pass petitions; take part in a demonstration; make and hold signs; listen to candidates speak and debate; attend city council meetings; attend school board meetings.

Farmers' Rally Primary Source Connection (page 81)

1. Farmers drove their tractors to or in Washington DC during a nighttime rally to make a statement about farm laws.
2. Answers will vary: sad, excited, lonely, afraid, proud, angry, determined, etc.
3. The media might have ran newspaper articles, spread the word through radio advertisements, posting fliers in cities, or running stories on television.
4. Answers will vary.

Join the Triangle Party Rally (page 82)

Students' answers will vary.

Join the Square Party Rally (page 83)

Students' answers will vary.

Making a Difference Comprehension Check (page 84)

Students' answers will vary.

The History of Voting Content-Area Vocabulary (page 88)

1. right
2. polls
3. responsibility
4. amendment
5. casts a vote
6. citizen

The History of Voting Graphic Organizer (page 90)

15th Amendment: 1870; non-whites; a person of any race or color could vote

19th Amendment: 1920; women; women could vote

26th Amendment: 1971; people between the ages of 18 and 20; it lowered the voting age to 18 (instead of 21)

1. calculate: present year–1971
2. Answers will vary
3. It is the law.
4. It is something American citizens should do.

Women Voters Primary Source Connection (pages 91–92)

1. It shows women being responsible citizens as they exercise their right to vote.
2. It said "a person" of any race or color. Women are people.
3. The 19th Amendment was ratified.
4. Answers will vary.

The Rights and Responsibilities of Voting (page 93)

1. Voting is a right because it is the law. Voting is a responsibility because it is something American citizens should do.
2. One-third fewer people vote in non presidential elections than in presidential elections; Texas and New York have lower voter turnouts than the nation does; Florida has higher voter turnouts than the nation.
3. Answers will vary.
4. Answers will vary.

The History of Voting Comprehension Check (page 94)

Students' answers will vary.

Answer Key *(cont.)*

Going to the Polls Content-Area Vocabulary (page 99)

Students' responses and illustrations will vary.

Going to the Polls Activity Sheet (page 101)

November 2000–November 9th
November 2004–November 6th
November 2008–November 5th
November 2012–November 4th
Students' lists of values and traits will vary.

Taking the Oath of Office Primary Source (pages 102–103)

1. Chester A. Arthur is taking the Oath of Office. It is being administered by Supreme Court Justice Brady. Arthur's hand is on a Bible. Other men are standing around, witnessing the swearing-in.
2. They look concerned.
3. Answers will vary.
4. The Oath has the president swear to preserve, protect, and defend the Constitution.

Candidate Values and Traits (page 104)

Mrs. E (possible traits): determined; responsible; confident; persuasive; thrifty; smart; quick thinker; sly; cunning; deceitful; self-reliant

Mr. J (possible traits): traditional; powerful; leader; determined; persuasive; flexible; quiet; shy; likable; opportunistic; hard-working; caring; generous

Going to the Polls Comprehension Check (page 108)

Students' answers will vary.

Elected Leaders in Action Content-Area Vocabulary (page 113)

Student comparisons will vary, but should be logical.

Elected Leaders in Action Graphic Organizer (page 115)

Executive Branch: runs congressional meetings; makes sure laws are obeyed; makes important decisions; signs bills into law; vetoes laws; works with world leaders; makes treaties; heads the military; mobilizes troops

Legislative Branch: makes laws; passes bills; approves treaties; approves a declaration of war

1. The president cannot make a new law until it has gone through Congress; the president cannot make big changes without congressional approval.
2. The president must sign bills into law and make big decisions for them to become approved.
3. Answers will vary.

Lincoln with His Cabinet Primary Source Connection (page 117)

1. Answers will vary.
2. Answers will vary.
3. Answers will vary.

Leadership from the Triangle/Square Party (page 118 or page 120)

1. president
2. Congress
3. president
4. Answers will vary.
5. Answers will vary.
6. Answers will vary.

Elected Leaders in Action Comprehension Check (page 122)

Students' answers will vary.

Doing My Part Content-Area Vocabulary (page 126)

Students' illustrations and sentences will vary.

Doing My Part Graphic Organizer (page 128)

Volunteer: Examples may include volunteering at a hospital, school, library, fire department, shelter, food pantry, zoo, fundraising campaign, neighborhood cleanup, YMCA, etc.

Jobs: Examples may include policeman, fireman, teacher, city worker, utility worker, road maintenance, etc.

Organizations: Examples may include Scouts, 4H, nonprofit organizations such as Kids Helping Kids, community organizations such as Friends of the Library, etc.

Answer Key *(cont.)*

Volunteering on the Home Front Primary Source Connection (pages 129–130)

1. The government challenged 100,000 people to come forward to volunteer as a nurse's aide. These women stepped up.

2. They performed tasks that nurses and doctors did not have time for, but were essential for a smooth-running hospital.

3. Possible Answer: Sick and injured people who came to the hospital may not have gotten the best care because the doctors and nurses would not have had the right equipment ready, or they would have been busy with other patients.

Collaborate to Succeed (page 131)

Situation 1

1. school board members; business owners; school leaders

2. The school board wants to reduce printing costs. Business owners will lose profits if the school board contracts with the local prison for printing. Schools may not get their printing in time.

3. local business owners

4. The school board goes with the prison contract.

5. business owners, by losing profits.

6. The school board goes with local businesses.

7. the school board, by not reducing expenses.

Situation 2

1. sheriff; state House and Senate leaders; governor

2. Police officers do not have access to juvenile records, so they do not know if wrong doers have been stopped before. The governor is concerned for the privacy rights of the state's citizens.

3. juvenile private citizens

4. The governor never signs a bill allowing policemen to have access to juvenile records.

5. policemen who do not know whether people have been in trouble before.

6. The governor signs a new bill allowing policemen to have access to juvenile records.

7. juvenile citizens, by revoking privacy rights.

Doing My Part Comprehension Check (page 132)

Students' answers will vary.

References Cited

Brookbank, D., S. Grover, K. Kullber, and C. Strawser. 1999. *Improving student achievement through organization of students learning.* Chicago: Master's Action Research Project, Saint Xavier University and IRI/Skylight.

Carnegie Corporation of New York and The Center for Information and Research on Civic Learning and Engagement. 2003. The civic mission of schools. http://www.civicmissionofschools.org/campaign/documents/CivicMissionofSchools.pdf (accessed on July 3, 2007).

Center for Civic Education. 1997. *National standards for civics and government.*

Chapman, C., M. J. Nolin, and K. Kline. 1997. *Student interest in national news and its relation to school courses* (NCES 97-970) U.S. Department of Education, National Center for Education Statistics. Washington, DC: U.S. Government Printing Office. http://nces.ed.gov/pubsearch/pubsinfo.asp?pubid=97970 (accessed on July 6, 2007).

Constitutional Rights Foundation. 2000. Fostering civic responsibility through service learning. *Service-Learning Network.* http://www.crf-usa.org/network/net8_1.html (accessed on July 5, 2007).

Hopkins, G. 1998. Why teach current events? *Education World.* http://www.educationworld.com/a_curr/curr084.shtml (accessed on July 6, 2007).

Kirlin, M. 2005. Promising approaches for strengthening civic education. White paper from the California Campaign for the Civic Mission of Schools http://www.cms-ca.org/CMS%20white%20paper%20final.pdf (accessed July 6, 2007).

Lutkus, A., and A. R. Weiss. 2007. *The nation's report card: Civics* 2006 (NCES 2007–476). U.S. Department of Education, National Center for Education Statistics. Washington, D.C.: U.S. Government Printing Office. http://nces.ed.gov/pubsearch/pubsinfo.asp?pubid=2007476 (accessed July 2, 2007).

Marzano, R. J., J. S. Norford, D. E. Paynter, D. J. Pickering, and B. B. Gaddy. 2001. *A handbook for classroom instruction that works.* Alexandria, VA: Association for Supervision & Curriculum Development.

Marzano, R. J., D. J. Pickering, and J. E. Pollock. 2001. *Classroom instruction that works: Research-based strategies for increasing student achievement.* Alexandria, VA: Association for Supervision and Curriculum Development.

National Council for the Social Studies. 1994. *Expectations of excellence: Curriculum standards for social studies.* Washington, DC: NCSS.

National Reading Panel. 2000. *Teaching children to read: An evidence-based assessment of the scientific research literature on reading and its implications for reading instruction.*

Olsen, K. 1995. Science continuum of concepts for grades K–6. Covington, WA: Books for Educators. http://www.nichd.nih.gov/publications/nrp/smallbooks.htm (accessed April 4, 2005).

Quigley, C. N. 2005. The civic mission of the schools: What constitutes an effective civic education? Paper presented at Education for Democracy: The Civic Mission of the Schools, Sacramento, CA.

Sinatra, R. C., J. Stahl-Glemake, and D. N. Berg. 1984. Improving reading comprehension of disabled readers through semantic mapping. *Reading Teaching* 38:22–29.

Stix, A. 2001. *Social studies strategies for active learning.* Huntington Beach, CA: Shell Education.

Additional Resources

The following resources were referenced when writing the background information pages:

Digital History. The presidency of Andrew Jackson. http://www.digitalhistory.uh.edu/database/article_display.cfm?HHID=637

Doherty, E. J. S. and L. C. Evans. 2000. Electing the president: Simulation similes. Chicago: Zephyr Press.

Fact Monster. Election day on Tuesdays? http://www.factmonster.com/spot/electionday1.html

Fair Vote. Past attempts at reform. http://www.fairvote.org/?page=979

Founder's Constitution, The. James Madison, federalist, no. 62, 415-22, article 1, section 3, clauses 1 and 2. http://press-pubs.uchicago.edu/founders/documents/a1_3_1-2s11.html

Franklin and Marshall College. Rendell's raiders. http://www.fandm.edu/x3902.xml.

Hamilton, A., J. Madison, and J. Jay. 1961. *The Federalist*. ed. Jacob E. Cooke. Middletown, CT: Wesleyan University Press.

Harper Week. Cartoon of the Day—The third-term panic. http://www.harpweek.com/09Cartoon/BrowseByDateCartoon.asp?Month=November&Date=7

Horn, G. 2004. *Political parties, interest groups, and the media*. Milwaukee, WI: World Almanac Library.

Johnston, R. D. 2002. *The making of America*. Washington, DC: National Geographic Society.

Joint Congressional Committee of Inaugural Ceremonies. Facts and firsts. http://inaugural.senate.gov/history/factsandfirsts/index.

Library of Congress for Teachers, The. The learning page: Elections… the American way. http://www.loc.gov/teachers/classroommaterials/presentationsandactivities/presentations/elections/home.html

Longley, R. "Why Third Parties?" About.com News & Issues http://usgovinfo.about.com/cs/politicalsystem/a/thirdparties.htm

McGuire, M. E. 1997. *Storypath: The presidential election sourcebook*. Seattle, WA: Everyday Learning Corporation.

Missouri General Assembly. Missouri revised statutes. Chapter 77, third class cities, section 77.230. http://www.moga.mo.gov/statutes/C000-099/0770000230.htm

Project Vote Smart. Government 101: Introduction. http://www.vote-smart.org/resource_govt101_01.php

Safire, W. 1972. "Origin of the elephant." In New language of politics. Rev. ed. New York: Collier Books.

U.S. National Archives and Records Administration. U.S. electoral college. http://www.archives.gov/federal-register/electoral-college

Elections Glossary

amendment—a law added to the constitution

ballot—a sheet of paper used to cast vote

campaign—an organized effort to achieve a specific goal, like getting elected

candidate—a person running for political office

cast a vote—to choose a candidate for office in an election

citizen—a person who lives in a city, state, or nation

collaborate—to work together; cooperate; act as a team

community—a group of people living in the same area and under the same government

Congress—the national legislative body of the United States that includes the Senate and the House of Representatives

conservative—to be careful and avoid giving freely

Constitution—laws written to show how the government will run

constitutional democracy—a system of government which limits the power of government, set forth in a constitution

debate—a discussion between two or more people in which ideas are given for or against issues

Democratic Party—the oldest political party in the United States, formed in 1792; one of the two main political parties today

demonstration—an organized protest by a group of people

Election Day—the day assigned for an election; polling day

elector—a citizen chosen to vote for the president and vice president of the United States

eligible—able to run for a political office

executive branch—the branch of the United States government that carries out laws

forum—a meeting where people openly discuss and debate issues

government—a system to rule a nation, state, town, or other group of people

governor—the leader of a state

Inauguration Day—the day the next United States president is sworn into office

influence—to persuade or sway someone to think or act differently

interest group—a group of people who strongly support similar ideas

issue—a matter for discussion or debate; a public concern

liberal—to be open-minded and to give away freely

mayor—the leader of a city or town

media—a way to report, write, edit, photograph, or otherwise show the news

nonprofit—not for making money; charitable

office—a position of authority, as in government

organization—a group of people that come together for a purpose

Elections Glossary *(cont.)*

petition—a written paper asking for a change

political party—a group whose members share the same ideas about government

politics—the act of being involved in government

poll—a place where people go to vote

public—a community of people; not private

qualify—to meet the rules to run for political office

rally—an organized assembly where people build enthusiasm for a cause

represent—stand in for; act for; be a symbol for

representative—a member of a state or national government; part of the House of Representatives

Republican Party—one of the two main political parties today; formed in 1854

responsibility—something someone should do; duty; obligation

right—something someone is entitled to do

run—to compete in a race for political office

senator—a member of state and national government; part of the Senate

strategy—a plan of action

term—the length of time of a political office

trait—a characteristic or quality of a person

treaty—a formal agreement between two or more governments

value—a principal or standard expected of people

veto—the power of the president to reject a bill passed by Congress; does not become law

volunteer—to do something of a person's own free will; unpaid worker

Contents of the Teacher Resource CD

Page(s)	Title	Filename
20	Political Parties Content-Area Vocabulary	politicalvocab.pdf
21	Political Parties Background Information	politicalbackinfo.pdf
22	Political Parties Graphic Organizer	politicalorganizer.pdf
23–24	Political Parties Primary Source Connection	politicalprimary.pdf
25–26	My Party Candidate	mycandidate.pdf
27	Political Parties Comprehension Check	politicalcomp.pdf
32	The Presidential Election Content-Area Vocabulary	presvocab.pdf
33	The Presidential Election Background Information	presbackinfo.pdf
34	The Presidential Election Graphic Organizer	presorganizer.pdf
35–36	The Constitution Rules Primary Source Connection	constitutionprimary.pdf
37	Who Is Eligible?	whoiseligible.pdf
38	The Presidential Election Comprehension Check	presidentialcomp.pdf
42	State and Local Elections Content-Area Vocabulary	statevocab.pdf
43	State and Local Leaders Background Information	statebackinfo.pdf
44	State and Local Leaders Graphic Organizer	stateorganizer.pdf
45–46	Mayor's Parade Primary Source Connection	mayorconnection.pdf
47	My State and Local Leaders	statelocalleaders.pdf
48	State and Local Elections Comprehension Check	statelocalcomp.pdf
52	The Candidates Content-Area Vocabulary	candidatesvocab.pdf
53	The Candidates Background Information	candidatesbackinfo.pdf
54	The Candidates Graphic Organizer	candidatesorganizer.pdf
55–56	James K. Polk: Presidential Candidate Primary Source Connection	polkprimary.pdf
57	Meet the Triangle Party Candidate	meettriangle.pdf
58	Meet the Square Party Candidate	meetsquare.pdf
59	The Candidates Comprehension Check	candidatescomp.pdf
64	On the Campaign Trail Content-Area Vocabulary	campaignvocab.pdf
65	On the Campaign Trail Background Information	campaignbackinfo.pdf
66	On the Campaign Trail Graphic Organizer	campaignorganizer.pdf
67–68	Campaign Craze Primary Source Connection	campaignprimary.pdf
69	My Triangle Party Candidate's Campaign	trianglecampaign.pdf
70	My Square Party Candidate's Campaign	squarecampaign.pdf
71	Campaign Contribution List	campaignlist.pdf
72	On the Campaign Trail Comprehension Check	campaigncomp.pdf
77	Making a Difference Content-Area Vocabulary	differencevocab.pdf

Contents of the Teacher Resource CD *(cont.)*

Page(s)	Title	Filename
78	Making a Difference Background Information	differencebackinfo.pdf
79	Making a Difference Graphic Organizer	differenceorganizer.pdf
80–81	Farmers' Rally Primary Source Connection	primaryconnection.pdf
82	Join the Triangle Party Rally	trianglerally.pdf
83	Join the Square Party Rally	squarerally.pdf
84	Making a Difference Comprehension Check	differencecomp.pdf
88	The History of Voting Content-Area Vocabulary	historyvocab.pdf
89	The History of Voting Background Information	historybackinfo.pdf
90	The History of Voting Graphic Organizer	historyorganizer.pdf
91–92	Women Voters Primary Source Connection	womenprimary.pdf
93	The Rights and Responsibilities of Voting	rightsvoting.pdf
94	The History of Voting Comprehension Check	historycomp.pdf
99	Going to the Polls Content-Area Vocabulary	pollsvocab.pdf
100	Going to the Polls Background Information	pollsbackinfo.pdf
101	Going to the Polls	pollsactivity.pdf
102–103	Taking the Oath of Office Primary Source Connection	takeoathprimary.pdf
104	Candidate Values and Traits	candidatevalues.pdf
105	Voter Application	voterapplication.pdf
106	Voter Identification Cards	votercards.pdf
107	Voting Ballots	votingballots.pdf
108	Going to the Polls Comprehension Check	pollscomp.pdf
113	Elected Leaders in Action Content-Area Vocabulary	leadersvocab.pdf
114	Elected Leaders in Action Background Information	leadersbackinfo.pdf
115	Elected Leaders in Action Graphic Organizer	leadersorganizer.pdf
116–117	Lincoln with His Cabinet Primary Source Connection	lincolnprimary.pdf
118–119	Leadership from the Triangle Party President	leadershiptriangle.pdf
120–121	Leadership from the Square Party President	leadershipsquare.pdf
122	Elected Leaders in Action Comprehension Check	leaderscomp.pdf
126	Doing My Part Content-Area Vocabulary	doingpartvocab.pdf
127	Doing My Part Background Information	doingpartbackinfo.pdf
128	Doing My Part Graphic Organizer	doingpartorganizer.pdf
129–130	Volunteering on the Home Front Primary Source Connection	homefrontprimary.pdf
131	Collaborate to Succeed	collaboratesucceed.pdf
132	Doing My Part Comprehension Check	doingpartcomp.pdf

Notes